Quick
400-Calorie
Favourites

Cataloguing data available from Bibliothèque et Archives nationales du Québec.

11-18

© 2018 Juniper Publishing, a division of Sogides Group Inc., a subsidiary of Quebecor Media Inc. (Montreal, Quebec)

Legal deposit: 2018
Bibliothèque et Archives nationales du Québec
Library and Archives Canada

ISBN 978-1-988002-88-0

Printed in Canada

**EXCLUSIVE DISTRIBUTOR
FOR CANADA & USA**

Simon & Schuster Canada
166 King Street East, Suite 300
Toronto ON M5A 1J3

Tel: 647-427-8882
Toll Free: 800-387-0446
Fax: 647-430-9446

simonandschuster.ca
canadianliving.com/books

Government of Quebec – Tax credit for book publishing – Administered by SODEC. **sodec.gouv.qc.ca**

This publisher gratefully acknowledges the support of the Société de développement des enterprises culturelles du Québec.

 Canada Council   Conseil des arts
for the Arts   du Canada

We gratefully acknowledge the support of the Canada Council for the Arts for its publishing program.

We acknowledge the financial support of our publishing activities by the Government of Canada through the Canada Book Fund.

ART DIRECTOR
Colin Elliott

EDITOR
Martin Zibauer

COPY EDITOR
Ruth Hanley

INDEXER
Lisa Fielding

Canadian Living

THE ESSENTIAL COLLECTION

Quick 400-Calorie Favourites

90+ TESTED-TILL-PERFECT RECIPES
FROM THE CANADIAN LIVING TEST KITCHEN

JUNIPER
PUBLISHING
A Quebecor Media Corporation

Welcome to the
Canadian Living Test Kitchen

Like you, we aim for balance in our lives. Canadians tell us they're looking for simple, nutritious recipes that are satisfying and mindful of calories without sacrificing flavour. In the Test Kitchen, we consider how best to combine our love of great food with our need to eat wisely. The secret isn't crash diets or other extremes, but eating a little bit better in our everyday meals. Whether you want healthier weekday options, are focused on weight management or want to offset an indulgent holiday, you'll find the recipes you need in this collection. We've included helpful side-dish suggestions to round out meals, plus a section of desserts under 200 calories—because balanced eating can include a few extras without blowing the calorie budget.

What Does Tested Till Perfect Mean?

Every year, the food specialists in the Canadian Living Test Kitchen work together to produce approximately 500 Tested-Till-Perfect recipes. So what does Tested Till Perfect mean? It means we follow a rigorous process to ensure you'll get the same results in your kitchen as we do in ours.

Here's What We Do:

- In the Test Kitchen, we use the same everyday ingredients and equipment commonly found in kitchens across Canada.

- We start by researching ideas and brainstorming as a team.

- We write up the recipe and go straight into the kitchen to try it out.

- We taste, evaluate and tweak the recipe until we really love it.

- Once developed, each recipe gets handed off to other food specialists for more testing and another tasting session.

- We meticulously test and retest each recipe as many times as it takes to make sure it turns out as perfectly in your kitchen as it does in ours.

- We carefully weigh and measure all ingredients, record the data and send the recipe for nutritional analysis.

- The recipe is then edited and rechecked to ensure all the information is correct and it's ready for you to cook.

TESTED
TILL
PERFECT
Canadian Living
TEST KITCHEN

Contents

MAKES 4 SERVINGS
HANDS-ON TIME 20 MINUTES
TOTAL TIME 20 MINUTES

One-Pan Tuscan Chicken

12	mini yellow-fleshed potatoes, halved
2	boneless skinless chicken breasts (about 450 g total)
½ tsp	each salt, pepper and garlic powder
⅓ cup	all-purpose flour
3 tbsp	unsalted butter, divided
1	sweet yellow pepper, cut in chunks
quarter	large red onion, sliced
2 cups	cherry tomatoes
½ cup	dry white wine
1 cup	sodium-reduced chicken broth
20	pitted Kalamata olives
½ cup	loosely packed fresh basil leaves
¼ cup	shaved Parmesan cheese

Place potatoes in microwaveable bowl; cover and microwave on high until tender, 3 to 5 minutes. Set aside.

Place 1 chicken breast on cutting board. Holding knife blade parallel to board and with opposite hand on top of chicken, slice horizontally all the way through breast to form 2 thin cutlets; repeat with remaining breast. Place chicken between 2 pieces of plastic wrap or waxed paper; use meat mallet or bottom of heavy pan to flatten chicken to even thickness. Sprinkle both sides with salt, pepper and garlic powder. Dredge in flour; shake off excess.

In large skillet, melt 1 tbsp butter over medium-high heat; cook chicken, turning once, until golden, 2 to 3 minutes. Transfer to plate.

In same pan, reduce heat to medium and melt remaining 2 tbsp butter. Add yellow pepper and onion; cook, stirring often, for 1 minute. Add tomatoes; cook for 1 minute more. Add wine, scraping up browned bits. Add broth; bring to boil. Nestle chicken into pan along with olives and potatoes. Reduce heat to medium and simmer, stirring often and turning chicken, until chicken is no longer pink inside and sauce has thickened slightly, 5 to 8 minutes. Sprinkle with basil and Parmesan.

NUTRITIONAL INFORMATION PER SERVING about 349 cal, 27 g pro, 16 g total fat (7 g sat. fat), 22 g carb (3 g dietary fibre, 5 g sugar), 81 mg chol, 1,064 mg sodium, 811 mg potassium. % RDI: 7% calcium, 12% iron, 16% vit A, 133% vit C, 15% folate.

TEST KITCHEN TIP

Flattening the chicken cutlets helps them cook quickly and evenly. If you like, swap out chicken for turkey.

Rosemary &
Chili Chicken Cutlets

MAKES 4 SERVINGS
HANDS-ON TIME 15 MINUTES
TOTAL TIME 15 MINUTES

In bowl, stir together wine, rosemary, hot pepper flakes, lemon zest and garlic. Add up to ¼ tsp more hot pepper flakes, if desired.

Place 1 chicken breast on cutting board. Holding knife blade parallel to board and with opposite hand on top of chicken, slice horizontally all the way through breast to form 2 thin cutlets; repeat with remaining breast. Sprinkle each with salt.

In nonstick skillet, heat oil over high heat; cook chicken, turning once, until golden, 5 to 8 minutes. Transfer to warmed plate; tent with foil. Reduce heat to medium; add wine mixture. Cook, scraping bottom of pan, until wine is reduced by half, 2 to 3 minutes. Remove from heat; gradually swirl in butter until blended. Drizzle sauce over chicken.

NUTRITIONAL INFORMATION PER SERVING about 250 cal, 26 g pro, 14 g total fat (6 g sat. fat), 1 g carb (trace dietary fibre, trace sugar), 88 mg chol, 269 mg sodium, 356 mg potassium. % RDI: 1% calcium, 4% iron, 8% vit A, 3% vit C, 1% folate.

½ cup	dry white wine (such as Sauvignon Blanc)
1 tsp	chopped fresh rosemary
¼ tsp	hot pepper flakes (approx)
1 tsp	lemon zest
1	clove garlic, finely grated or pressed
2	boneless skinless chicken breasts (about 450 g total)
¼ tsp	salt
1 tbsp	olive oil
3 tbsp	cold butter, cut in cubes

MAKE IT A MEAL

Rosemary & Chili Chicken Cutlets	250 cal
Add: ½ cup cooked white long-grain rice	103 cal
Total	**353 cal**

Asparagus & Chicken Piccata
With Herbed Couscous

MAKES 4 SERVINGS
HANDS-ON TIME 15 MINUTES
TOTAL TIME 15 MINUTES

PICCATA

450 g	boneless skinless chicken breast cutlets
¼ tsp	each salt and pepper, divided
2 tbsp	all-purpose flour, divided
1 tbsp	olive oil, divided
1	bunch asparagus (about 450 g), trimmed and cut in 2-inch lengths
1 tbsp	butter
½ cup	dry white wine
1 cup	sodium-reduced chicken broth
1 tbsp	capers, drained and rinsed
1 tbsp	lemon juice

HERBED COUSCOUS

¼ cup	couscous
pinch	each salt and pepper
1 cup	boiling water
¼ cup	chopped fresh parsley
2 tsp	lemon juice

PICCATA Sprinkle chicken with pinch each of the salt and pepper. Sprinkle with 1 tbsp of the flour, turning to coat both sides and shaking off excess. In nonstick skillet, heat 2 tsp of the oil over medium-high heat; cook chicken, turning once, until golden, about 4 minutes. Transfer to plate.

In same pan, heat remaining 1 tsp oil over medium heat; cook asparagus, stirring occasionally, until tender-crisp, about 3 minutes. Transfer to plate.

In same pan, melt butter over medium heat. Gradually whisk in remaining 1 tbsp flour; cook, stirring, for 1 minute. Pour in wine; bring to boil over medium heat. Cook, stirring, until reduced by half, about 1 minute.

Pour in broth; bring to boil. Add chicken; cook, stirring until chicken is no longer pink inside and sauce has thickened, about 3 minutes. Stir in capers, lemon juice and remaining salt and pepper. Stir in asparagus.

HERBED COUSCOUS While chicken is cooking, in heatproof bowl, whisk together couscous, salt and pepper; pour in boiling water. Cover tightly with plastic wrap; let stand until no liquid remains, about 5 minutes. Fluff with fork. Stir in parsley and lemon juice. Serve with piccata.

NUTRITIONAL INFORMATION PER SERVING about 339 cal, 32 g pro, 8 g total fat (3 g sat. fat), 29 g carb (2 g dietary fibre, 2 g sugar), 74 mg chol, 454 mg sodium, 554 mg potassium. % RDI: 4% calcium, 14% iron, 12% vit A, 17% vit C, 51% folate.

TEST KITCHEN TIP

Some brands of regular packaged broth can be too salty for many recipes. In the Test Kitchen, we generally prefer cooking with sodium-reduced broth, which gives us more control over a recipe's flavour and sodium content. It's always easier to add a little salt to a dish, if needed, than it is to remove it.

Quick Chicken & Edamame Stir-Fry

MAKES 4 SERVINGS
HANDS-ON TIME 25 MINUTES
TOTAL TIME 25 MINUTES

In saucepan of boiling salted water, cook edamame for 1 minute; drain. Set aside.

In wok or large nonstick skillet, heat oil over medium-high heat; stir-fry ginger and garlic until fragrant, about 30 seconds. Add chicken; stir-fry until lightly browned, about 5 minutes.

Add red pepper and edamame; stir-fry until vegetables are slightly softened, about 2 minutes. Stir in hoisin and oyster sauces; stir-fry until vegetables are coated and chicken is no longer pink inside, about 1 minute.

1 cup	frozen shelled edamame
2 tsp	vegetable oil
2 tsp	minced fresh ginger
2	cloves garlic, minced
450 g	boneless skinless chicken thighs, cut in 1-inch chunks
1	sweet red pepper, thinly sliced
2 tbsp	hoisin sauce
1 tbsp	oyster sauce

NUTRITIONAL INFORMATION PER SERVING about 234 cal, 26 g pro, 10 g total fat (2 g sat. fat), 10 g carb (2 g dietary fibre, 4 g sugar), 94 mg chol, 426 mg sodium, 472 mg potassium. % RDI: 4% calcium, 15% iron, 10% vit A, 90% vit C, 50% folate.

MAKE IT A MEAL

Quick Chicken & Edamame Stir-Fry	234 cal
Add: ½ cup cooked white long-grain rice	103 cal
Total	**337 cal**

MAKES 2 SERVINGS
HANDS-ON TIME 20 MINUTES
TOTAL TIME 20 MINUTES

Skillet Mediterranean Chicken

1	large boneless skinless chicken breast (about 225 g)
½ tsp	dried tarragon
½ tsp	dried oregano
¼ tsp	each salt and pepper
1 tbsp	olive oil, divided
85 g	Broccolini
half	sweet yellow pepper, coarsely chopped
2	cloves garlic, minced
2 tbsp	chopped pitted Kalamata olives
¼ cup	dry white wine
¼ cup	crumbled feta cheese
1 tbsp	chopped fresh basil

Place chicken breast on cutting board. Holding knife blade parallel to board and with opposite hand on top of chicken, slice horizontally all the way through breast to form 2 thin cutlets. Sprinkle both sides of each with tarragon, oregano, salt and pepper.

In large nonstick skillet, heat 1 tsp of the oil over medium-high heat; cook chicken, turning once, until lightly browned, about 4 minutes. Transfer to plate.

In same pan, heat remaining 2 tsp oil over medium-high heat; cook Broccolini, yellow pepper, garlic and olives until fragrant, about 2 minutes. Add chicken and wine; cover and simmer until chicken is no longer pink inside and Broccolini is tender-crisp, 4 to 5 minutes. Remove from heat; sprinkle with feta and basil.

NUTRITIONAL INFORMATION PER SERVING about 289 cal, 31 g pro, 14 g total fat (5 g sat. fat), 10 g carb (2 g dietary fibre, 3 g sugar), 83 mg chol, 1,009 mg sodium, 646 mg potassium. % RDI: 15% calcium, 14% iron, 12% vit A, 160% vit C, 19% folate.

TEST KITCHEN TIP

Broccolini is a hybrid of gailan (sometimes called Chinese broccoli) and broccoli. If you don't have Broccolini, try substituting broccoli florets or asparagus. Serve this dish with a side of orzo or couscous to round out the meal.

Maple-Mustard Chicken Thighs
With Lemon-Broccoli Couscous

MAKES 4 SERVINGS
HANDS-ON TIME 25 MINUTES
TOTAL TIME 25 MINUTES

MAPLE-MUSTARD CHICKEN In small bowl, whisk together mustard, maple syrup, vinegar and sesame oil. Set aside. *(Make-ahead: Cover and refrigerate for up to 24 hours.)*

Sprinkle chicken with salt and pepper. In nonstick skillet, heat olive oil over medium heat; cook chicken, turning once, until golden and no longer pink inside and juices run clear when thickest part is pierced, about 10 minutes. Transfer chicken to plate; tent with foil.

Drain fat from pan; reduce heat to medium-low. Add mustard mixture; cook, stirring and scraping up browned bits, until slightly thickened, about 30 seconds. Return chicken to pan; cook, stirring, until glazed and heated through, about 2 minutes.

LEMON-BROCCOLI COUSCOUS While chicken is cooking, in heatproof bowl, whisk couscous with salt; pour in boiling water. Cover tightly with plastic wrap; let stand until no liquid remains, about 5 minutes. Fluff with fork.

Meanwhile, in small saucepan of boiling water, cook broccoli until tender-crisp, about 1 minute; drain. Stir into couscous. Stir in lemon zest and lemon juice. Serve with chicken. Sprinkle with sesame seeds.

NUTRITIONAL INFORMATION PER SERVING about 313 cal, 27 g pro, 9 g total fat (2 g sat. fat), 31 g carb (2 g dietary fibre, 7 g sugar), 93 mg chol, 551 mg sodium, 474 mg potassium. % RDI: 5% calcium, 16% iron, 12% vit A, 40% vit C, 17% folate.

MAPLE-MUSTARD CHICKEN

3 tbsp	Dijon mustard
2 tbsp	maple syrup
4 tsp	balsamic vinegar
¼ tsp	sesame oil
450 g	boneless skinless chicken thighs
¼ tsp	each salt and pepper
2 tsp	olive oil

LEMON-BROCCOLI COUSCOUS

⅔ cup	couscous
¼ tsp	salt
1 cup	boiling water
2 cups	bite-size broccoli florets
½ tsp	grated lemon zest
1 tsp	lemon juice
1 tsp	sesame seeds, toasted

TEST KITCHEN TIP

Running late? You can use frozen broccoli in the couscous; frozen broccoli is often cheaper than fresh, and precut florets will cut down on prep time.

MAKES 10 TO 12 SERVINGS
HANDS-ON TIME 30 MINUTES
TOTAL TIME 1½ HOURS

Sweet Potato & Chicken Chili

1 tbsp	canola oil
1 kg	lean ground chicken
6	ribs celery, diced
2	onions, diced
2	sweet green peppers, diced
1	sweet potato, peeled and grated
2	796 ml cans diced or stewed tomatoes
2	400 ml cans sodium-reduced mixed beans, drained and rinsed
⅓ cup	white vinegar
2 tbsp	Dijon mustard
2 tbsp	chili powder
1 tbsp	dried oregano
2 tsp	salt
½ tsp	pepper

In Dutch oven or large heavy-bottomed pot, heat oil over medium-high heat; cook chicken, breaking up with spoon, until no longer pink, about 5 minutes.

Stir in celery, onions, green peppers, sweet potato, tomatoes, beans, vinegar, mustard, chili powder, oregano, salt and pepper. Reduce heat to medium; cover and simmer, stirring often, for 1 hour. (Chili will thicken as it sits.)

NUTRITIONAL INFORMATION PER EACH OF 12 SERVINGS about 152 cal, 12 g pro, 8 g total fat (2 g sat. fat), 16 g carb (4 g dietary fibre, 4 g sugar), 41 mg chol, 474 mg sodium, 299 mg potassium. % RDI: 8% calcium, 16% iron, 32% vit A, 43% vit C, 6% folate.

TEST KITCHEN TIP

If you like, top each bowl of chili with a small dollop of sour cream, some shredded cheddar and sliced green onions.

Chicken & Kale Stew
With Chili Yogurt

MAKES 6 SERVINGS
HANDS-ON TIME 30 MINUTES
TOTAL TIME 30 MINUTES

CHICKEN & KALE STEW In Dutch oven or large heavy-bottomed pot, heat oil over medium-high heat; cook squash and onion, stirring occasionally, until onion is beginning to brown, about 4 minutes. Add garlic, chili pepper and ginger; cook, stirring, for 1 minute.

Stir in broth, sage, thyme, pepper and salt; bring to boil. Reduce heat and simmer, stirring occasionally, for 5 minutes. Add chicken; simmer, stirring occasionally, for 5 minutes.

Using slotted spoon, transfer chili pepper to cutting board; mince chili pepper. Reserve for Chili Yogurt.

Add kale and corn to pot; cook, stirring occasionally, until kale is wilted and chicken is no longer pink inside, about 2 minutes. Stir in lemon juice.

Whisk cornstarch with water; stir into pot. Bring to boil; cook, stirring, until thickened, about 1 minute. Ladle stew into serving bowls. Sprinkle with sunflower seeds.

CHILI YOGURT In small bowl, stir together yogurt, chives, lemon juice and reserved chili pepper; dollop over stew.

NUTRITIONAL INFORMATION PER SERVING about 195 cal, 23 g pro, 4 g total fat (1 g sat. fat), 18 g carb (3 g dietary fibre, 4 g sugar), 44 mg chol, 532 mg sodium, 588 mg potassium. % RDI: 8% calcium, 11% iron, 94% vit A, 50% vit C, 15% folate.

CHICKEN & KALE STEW

1 tsp	olive oil
2½ cups	cubed seeded peeled butternut squash
1	onion, thinly sliced
2	cloves garlic, finely grated or pressed
1	small finger chili pepper (red or yellow), halved lengthwise and seeded
1 tbsp	minced peeled fresh ginger
1	900 ml pkg sodium-reduced chicken broth
½ tsp	each dried sage and dried thyme
½ tsp	pepper
¼ tsp	salt
450 g	boneless skinless chicken breasts, cubed
4 cups	chopped stemmed kale
½ cup	frozen corn kernels
1 tsp	lemon juice
2 tbsp	cornstarch
2 tbsp	water
2 tbsp	sunflower seeds, toasted

CHILI YOGURT

⅓ cup	2% Greek yogurt
1 tbsp	chopped fresh chives
½ tsp	lemon juice

Slow Cooker
Chicken Tikka Masala

MAKES 8 SERVINGS
HANDS-ON TIME 15 MINUTES
COOKING TIME 8 HOURS
TOTAL TIME 8¼ HOURS

CHICKEN TIKKA MASALA

1	796 ml can diced tomatoes
1	156 ml can tomato paste
1½ cups	sliced sweet onion (about 1 small)
⅔ cup	water
2 tbsp	packed brown sugar
1 tbsp	finely chopped fresh ginger
3	cloves garlic, finely chopped
2 tsp	each ground cumin and garam masala
1 tsp	paprika
½ tsp	each salt and turmeric
pinch	cayenne pepper
900 g	boneless skinless chicken breasts, cut in 1-inch chunks
¼ cup	35% cream
1 tbsp	lemon juice

CUCUMBER RAITA

1 cup	grated peeled cucumber (about half cucumber)
pinch	salt
1 cup	Balkan-style yogurt
¼ cup	chopped fresh cilantro
2 tsp	lemon juice

CHICKEN TIKKA MASALA In slow cooker, combine tomatoes, tomato paste, onion, water, brown sugar, ginger, garlic, cumin, garam masala, paprika, salt, turmeric and cayenne pepper. Cover and cook on low for 8 to 10 hours.

Using immersion blender, purée tomato mixture until smooth. Add chicken; cover and cook on high until chicken is no longer pink inside, about 30 minutes. Stir in cream and lemon juice. *(Make-ahead: Cover and refrigerate for up to 24 hours. Reheat before serving.)*

CUCUMBER RAITA While chicken is cooking, in colander, sprinkle cucumber with salt; let stand for 5 minutes. Squeeze out excess liquid and pat dry.

In small bowl, stir together cucumber, yogurt, cilantro and lemon juice. *(Make-ahead: Cover and refrigerate for up to 24 hours.)* Serve with Chicken Tikka Masala.

NUTRITIONAL INFORMATION PER SERVING about 239 cal, 29 g pro, 7 g total fat (3 g sat. fat), 17 g carb (3 g dietary fibre, 10 g sugar), 80 mg chol, 379 mg sodium, 882 mg potassium. % RDI: 10% calcium, 21% iron, 11% vit A, 37% vit C, 8% folate.

MAKE IT A MEAL

Slow Cooker Chicken Tikka Masala	239 cal
Add: ½ cup cooked brown basmati rice	108 cal
Total	**347 cal**

Cold Peanut Chicken Rolls

MAKES 6 SERVINGS
HANDS-ON TIME 35 MINUTES
TOTAL TIME 35 MINUTES

PEANUT DIPPING SAUCE In bowl, stir together peanut butter, soy sauce, water, brown sugar, vinegar and chili sauce until creamy. *(Make-ahead: Refrigerate in airtight container for up to 2 days.)* Transfer one-third of the sauce to separate bowl; set aside.

Scrape remaining sauce into serving bowl; top with green onions (if using) and sesame seeds.

CHICKEN ROLLS Stir reserved dipping sauce into quinoa; set aside.

Fill 9-inch pie plate with hot water. Working with 1 rice paper wrapper at a time, soak in hot water until soft, 5 to 10 seconds; transfer to kitchen towel and lightly pat to remove excess water.

Place 2 tsp cilantro in centre of each wrapper; spoon 2 tbsp quinoa mixture over top. Layer with a few pieces each of cucumber, carrot, red pepper and avocado. Top with scant ¼ cup chicken.

Fold bottom over filling; fold in sides and roll up. Place on damp kitchen towel–lined baking sheet; cover with another damp kitchen towel to prevent drying out. Repeat with remaining ingredients to make 12 rolls. *(Make-ahead: Refrigerate for up to 6 hours.)* Serve with dipping sauce.

NUTRITIONAL INFORMATION PER SERVING about 329 cal, 20 g pro, 12 g total fat (3 g sat. fat), 35 g carb (4 g dietary fibre, 7 g sugar), 46 mg chol, 415 mg sodium, 493 mg potassium. % RDI: 3% calcium, 15% iron, 35% vit A, 48% vit C, 27% folate.

PEANUT DIPPING SAUCE

3 tbsp	smooth peanut butter
2 tbsp	sodium-reduced soy sauce
2 tbsp	water
1 tbsp	packed brown sugar
1 tbsp	rice vinegar
1 tsp	Asian chili sauce (such as sriracha)
¼ cup	chopped green onions (optional)
1 tsp	sesame seeds

CHICKEN ROLLS

1½ cups	cooked quinoa
	hot water
12	rice paper wrappers (9 inches)
½ cup	fresh cilantro
1 cup	each julienned English cucumber and carrot
1	sweet red pepper, thinly sliced
1	avocado, peeled, pitted and thinly sliced
2 cups	shredded cooked chicken

TEST KITCHEN TIP

Have a few extra rice paper wrappers for backup—once soaked, the wrappers are fragile and rip easily. Be careful not to add too much filling to each wrapper; they'll become difficult to roll tightly and neatly.

MAKES 4 SERVINGS
HANDS-ON TIME 15 MINUTES
TOTAL TIME 15 MINUTES

Curried Chicken Skewers
With Creamy Chickpea Salad

CURRIED CHICKEN

2 tbsp	Balkan-style yogurt
1 tbsp	mild curry paste
2	cloves garlic, grated or pressed
pinch	salt
450 g	boneless skinless chicken breasts, cut in 24 cubes

CHICKPEA SALAD

¼ cup	Balkan-style yogurt
¼ cup	light mayonnaise
1½ tsp	grated fresh ginger
1	small clove garlic, pressed or grated
pinch	each salt and pepper
1	can (540 ml) chickpeas, drained, rinsed and patted dry
1 cup	finely chopped cucumber
¼ cup	chopped fresh cilantro
2	green onions, sliced
1	rib celery, diced

CURRIED CHICKEN In bowl, stir together yogurt, curry paste, garlic and salt; add chicken and stir to coat. Thread 3 pieces of the chicken onto each of 8 metal or soaked wooden skewers. Place on greased grill over medium-high heat; close lid and grill, turning once, until no longer pink inside, about 8 minutes.

CHICKPEA SALAD Meanwhile, in large bowl, whisk together yogurt, mayonnaise, ginger, garlic, salt and pepper. Add chickpeas, cucumber, cilantro, green onions and celery; stir to coat. Serve with chicken.

NUTRITIONAL INFORMATION PER SERVING about 331 cal, 33 g pro, 12 g total fat (2 g sat. fat), 24 g carb (6 g dietary fibre, 5 g sugar), 75 mg chol, 449 mg sodium, 555 mg potassium. % RDI: 8% calcium, 11% iron, 5% vit A, 7% vit C, 21% folate.

Grilled Sesame Chicken & Radish Skewers
With Orange Salad

MAKES 4 SERVINGS
HANDS-ON TIME 30 MINUTES
TOTAL TIME 30 MINUTES

CHICKEN & RADISH SKEWERS In bowl, whisk together honey, soy sauce, sesame oil and garlic. Set aside.

Sprinkle chicken with ½ tsp of the salt and the pepper. Thread 3 pieces of the chicken onto each of eight 6-inch metal or soaked wooden skewers. Place on greased grill over medium-high heat; close lid and grill, turning once, until no longer pink inside, about 8 minutes. Brush with some of the honey mixture; grill, turning and brushing with some of the remaining honey mixture halfway through, for 1 minute. Transfer skewers to plate; sprinkle with 2 tsp of the sesame seeds.

While chicken is grilling, thread 3 of the radishes onto each of four 6-inch metal or soaked wooden skewers. Place on greased grill over medium-high heat; close lid and grill, turning once, until tender and slightly charred, about 6 minutes. Brush with some of the remaining honey mixture; grill, turning and brushing with some of the remaining honey mixture halfway through, for 1 minute.

Remove radishes from skewers and place in bowl; drizzle with any remaining honey mixture. Sprinkle with remaining 1 tsp sesame seeds and ¼ tsp salt.

ORANGE SALAD Meanwhile, cut off zest and pith from orange; cut between membrane and pulp to release sections. Squeeze 1 tsp juice from remaining membranes into large bowl. Set sections aside.

Whisk oil, vinegar, honey, wasabi, salt and pepper into orange juice. *(Make-ahead: Refrigerate in airtight container for up to 24 hours.)* Add lettuce, avocado and reserved orange segments; gently toss to coat. Serve with chicken and radishes.

NUTRITIONAL INFORMATION PER SERVING about 326 cal, 28 g pro, 16 g total fat (3 g sat. fat), 19 g carb (5 g dietary fibre, 12 g sugar), 66 mg chol, 663 mg sodium, 755 mg potassium. % RDI: 4% calcium, 10% iron, 17% vit A, 35% vit C, 34% folate.

CHICKEN & RADISH SKEWERS

2 tbsp	liquid honey
1 tbsp	sodium-reduced soy sauce
1 tsp	sesame oil
1	clove garlic, finely grated or pressed
450 g	boneless skinless chicken breasts, cut in 24 cubes
¾ tsp	salt, divided
¼ tsp	pepper
12	small radishes, trimmed
1 tbsp	sesame seeds, toasted and divided

ORANGE SALAD

1	orange
4 tsp	extra-virgin olive oil
1 tsp	seasoned rice vinegar
½ tsp	liquid honey
½ tsp	prepared wasabi
pinch	each salt and pepper
4 cups	chopped green leaf lettuce
1	avocado, peeled, pitted and sliced

MAKES 4 TO 6 SERVINGS
HANDS-ON TIME 25 MINUTES
TOTAL TIME 50 MINUTES

Vietnamese Chopped Salad
With Grilled Chicken Skewers

CHILI LIME DRESSING

2 tbsp	lime juice
2 tbsp	rice wine vinegar
1 tbsp	packed brown sugar
1 tsp	toasted sesame oil
1 tsp	grated fresh ginger
1 tsp	sriracha
1	small chili, minced

VIETNAMESE CHOPPED SALAD

2	boneless skinless chicken breasts, sliced in ¼-inch thick strips
1	sweet red pepper, julienned
1	carrot, cut in ribbons
2 cups	julienned napa cabbage
1 cup	julienned red cabbage
2	heads baby bok choy, julienned
2	green onions, thinly sliced
½ cup	thinly sliced snow peas
1	ripe mango, peeled, pitted and thinly sliced
¼ cup	each fresh basil, cilantro and mint leaves
⅓ cup	roasted peanuts
¼ cup	fried shallots (optional)
	lime wedges (optional)

CHILI LIME DRESSING In small bowl, whisk together lime juice, vinegar, brown sugar, sesame oil, ginger, sriracha and chili. Set aside.

VIETNAMESE CHOPPED SALAD Toss chicken with 2 tbsp of the reserved dressing. Refrigerate for 30 minutes. Thread onto metal or soaked bamboo skewers. Place on greased grill over medium-high heat; close lid and grill, turning occasionally, until chicken is no longer pink inside, 5 to 7 minutes.

Meanwhile, in large bowl, toss together red pepper, carrot, napa cabbage, red cabbage and baby bok choy. Add green onions, snow peas, mango, basil, cilantro and mint. Toss gently and arrange on large platter with chicken skewers. Drizzle with remaining dressing. Sprinkle with peanuts and fried shallots (if using). Serve immediately, with lime wedges on the side (if using).

NUTRITIONAL INFORMATION PER EACH OF 6 SERVINGS about 168 cal, 15 g pro, 6 g total fat (1 g sat. fat), 17 g carb (3 g dietary fibre, 11 g sugar), 28 mg chol, 88 mg sodium, 577 mg potassium. % RDI: 8% calcium, 10% iron, 67% vit A, 140% vit C, 22% folate.

TEST KITCHEN TIP

Toasted sesame oil is pressed from toasted sesame seeds and has a deep golden colour. You need only a small amount to add rich, nutty flavour to a dish. Regular sesame oil, pressed from untoasted seeds, has a lighter colour, is more neutral in flavour and can be used for stir-frying.

Chicken Lettuce Cups

MAKES 4 SERVINGS
HANDS-ON TIME 20 MINUTES
TOTAL TIME 20 MINUTES

In large nonstick skillet, heat oil over medium heat; cook white parts of green onions, stirring, until softened, 1 to 2 minutes. Increase heat to medium-high. Stir in chicken and garlic; cook, breaking up chicken with spoon, until no longer pink, about 5 minutes.

Stir together hoisin sauce, soy sauce, vinegar and ginger; pour into chicken mixture. Cook, stirring occasionally, until sauce is slightly thickened, about 2 minutes. Remove from heat; stir in water chestnuts and green parts of green onions.

Arrange Boston lettuce on serving platter in single layer; top each leaf of Boston lettuce with 1 leaf of iceberg lettuce. Spoon chicken mixture into centres. Top with cucumbers, carrot and chili garlic sauce.

NUTRITIONAL INFORMATION PER SERVING about 378 cal, 23 g pro, 19 g total fat (5 g sat. fat), 28 g carb (4 g dietary fibre, 18 g sugar), 87 mg chol, 965 mg sodium, 444 mg potassium. % RDI: 7% calcium, 21% iron, 59% vit A, 20% vit C, 39% folate.

1 tbsp	canola oil
4	green onions, chopped (white and green parts separated)
450 g	ground chicken
3	cloves garlic, minced
⅓ cup	hoisin sauce
7 tsp	soy sauce
2 tbsp	rice vinegar
1 tbsp	finely grated fresh ginger
1	218 ml can water chestnuts, drained and chopped
12	leaves Boston lettuce
12	leaves iceberg lettuce
2	mini cucumbers, sliced
1 cup	julienned carrot
1 tbsp	chili garlic sauce

MAKES 4 SERVINGS
HANDS-ON TIME 20 MINUTES
TOTAL TIME 30 MINUTES

Chili Chicken Salad

8	boneless skinless chicken thighs
¼ tsp	each salt and pepper
2 tbsp	canola oil
1 tbsp	fish sauce
1 tbsp	white vinegar
2 tsp	sambal oelek or other chili paste
1 tsp	liquid honey
1	clove garlic, minced
4	carrots
4	cocktail tomatoes, cut in wedges
1	English cucumber, halved lengthwise and sliced crosswise
1 cup	fresh mint leaves, torn
1 cup	fresh cilantro leaves, torn
2	green onions, sliced
¼ cup	chopped unsalted roasted peanuts

Grease and preheat grill to medium-high. Sprinkle chicken all over with salt and pepper. Place on grill; close lid and grill, flipping once, until juices run clear when thickest part is pierced, 8 to 10 minutes. Transfer to cutting board; tent with foil. Let rest for 5 minutes before slicing.

Meanwhile, in large bowl, whisk together oil, fish sauce, vinegar, sambal oelek, honey and garlic.

Using vegetable peeler, shave carrots lengthwise into ribbons. Add chicken, carrots, tomatoes, cucumber, mint, cilantro and green onions to dressing; toss to coat. Divide among plates; sprinkle with peanuts.

NUTRITIONAL INFORMATION PER SERVING about 368 cal, 33 g pro, 20 g total fat (3 g sat. fat), 16 g carb (4 g dietary fibre, 8 g sugar), 126 mg chol, 700 mg sodium, 880 mg potassium. % RDI: 8% calcium, 23% iron, 133% vit A, 30% vit C, 26% folate.

Hoisin-Glazed Chicken
With Five-Spice Broth

MAKES 4 SERVINGS
HANDS-ON TIME 20 MINUTES
TOTAL TIME 30 MINUTES

Preheat oven to 400°F. In large nonstick skillet, heat 1 tsp of the oil over medium-high heat; cook chicken, turning once, until browned all over, about 8 minutes.

Transfer chicken to parchment paper–lined baking sheet; brush with hoisin sauce. Bake until no longer pink inside, 12 to 15 minutes. Let cool enough to handle; thinly slice and set aside.

Cook noodles according to package directions; drain and set aside.

Meanwhile, in large saucepan, heat remaining 1 tsp oil over medium heat; cook ginger, garlic, cilantro stems and five-spice powder, stirring, for 1 minute.

Add broth, water and soy sauce; bring to boil. Reduce heat and simmer for 5 minutes. Using slotted spoon, discard ginger, garlic and cilantro stems. Stir in bok choy; simmer until softened, 2 to 4 minutes.

To serve, divide noodles, bok choy, broth mixture and chicken among serving bowls. Sprinkle with green onions and chopped cilantro; drizzle with sesame oil.

NUTRITIONAL INFORMATION PER SERVING about 357 cal, 32 g pro, 6 g total fat (1 g sat. fat), 42 g carb (3 g dietary fibre, 4 g sugar), 66 mg chol, 948 mg sodium, 814 mg potassium. % RDI: 13% calcium, 16% iron, 52% vit A, 57% vit C, 29% folate.

2 tsp	vegetable oil, divided
450 g	boneless skinless chicken breasts
4 tsp	hoisin sauce
170 g	rice stick noodles (¼ inch wide)
8	thin slices fresh ginger
2	cloves garlic, thinly sliced
2	whole stems fresh cilantro (with roots)
¼ tsp	five-spice powder
1	900 ml pkg sodium-reduced chicken broth
2 cups	water
1 tbsp	sodium-reduced soy sauce
6	heads baby Shanghai bok choy, trimmed (root ends attached) and halved
2	green onions, thinly sliced
2 tbsp	chopped fresh cilantro
1 tsp	sesame oil

TEST KITCHEN TIP

Serve with lime wedges and Asian chili sauce, such as sriracha, on the side.

MAKES 4 SERVINGS
HANDS-ON TIME 20 MINUTES
TOTAL TIME 30 MINUTES

Curried Lentil & Chicken Soup

1 tbsp	olive oil, divided
450 g	boneless skinless chicken thighs, chopped
1	onion, diced
1	carrot, diced
4	cloves garlic, minced
2 tsp	curry powder
1 tsp	ground coriander
½ tsp	ground cumin
¼ tsp	salt
3 cups	sodium-reduced chicken broth
1 cup	dried red lentils, rinsed
1 tbsp	lemon juice
½ cup	Balkan-style yogurt
¼ cup	chopped fresh parsley or fresh cilantro

In Dutch oven or large heavy-bottomed pot, heat 1½ tsp of the oil over medium-high heat; cook chicken, stirring, until light golden, about 3 minutes. Transfer to plate; set aside.

In same pot, heat remaining 1½ tsp oil over medium heat; cook onion and carrot, stirring occasionally, until beginning to soften, about 3 minutes. Add garlic, curry powder, coriander, cumin and salt; cook, stirring, until fragrant, about 30 seconds. Stir in broth and lentils; bring to boil. Reduce heat, cover and simmer until lentils are tender, about 10 minutes.

Stir in chicken and any juices. Cook, uncovered and stirring occasionally, until slightly thickened and chicken is no longer pink inside, about 5 minutes. Remove from heat; stir in lemon juice. Spoon into serving bowls; top with yogurt and parsley.

NUTRITIONAL INFORMATION PER SERVING about 385 cal, 36 g pro, 11 g total fat (3 g sat. fat), 37 g carb (8 g dietary fibre, 6 g sugar), 89 mg chol, 708 mg sodium, 949 mg potassium. % RDI: 11% calcium, 48% iron, 39% vit A, 20% vit C, 123% folate.

TEST KITCHEN TIP

Chicken thighs are less expensive than breasts, and they give this robust soup added heartiness. If you don't have plain yogurt, top each bowl with light sour cream.

Skinny Turkey Bolognese

MAKES 6 SERVINGS
HANDS-ON TIME 35 MINUTES
TOTAL TIME 35 MINUTES

In large pot of boiling salted water, cook pasta according to package directions. Drain; set aside.

Meanwhile, in large skillet, heat oil over medium-high heat; cook carrots, celery and onion, stirring occasionally, until carrots are tender-crisp, 5 to 6 minutes. Add Italian seasoning, garlic powder and salt; cook for 1 minute. Add turkey and sun-dried tomatoes; cook, breaking up turkey with spoon, until turkey is beginning to brown, about 5 minutes.

Add crushed tomatoes and sugar; reduce heat to medium. Cover and simmer, stirring occasionally, for 8 minutes. Stir in spinach until wilted. Serve over pasta; sprinkle with nutritional yeast (if using).

NUTRITIONAL INFORMATION PER SERVING about 390 cal, 23 g pro, 12 g total fat (3 g sat. fat), 52 g carb (8 g dietary fibre, 12 g sugar), 60 mg chol, 559 mg sodium, 954 mg potassium. % RDI: 11% calcium, 36% iron, 63% vit A, 30% vit C, 24% folate.

250 g	whole wheat fettuccine
2 tbsp	olive oil
2	carrots, diced
2	ribs celery, diced
1	onion, chopped
1 tbsp	Italian herb seasoning
2 tsp	garlic powder
¼ tsp	salt
454 g	lean ground turkey
¼ cup	chopped oil-packed sun-dried tomatoes
1	796 ml can crushed tomatoes
1 tsp	granulated sugar
2 cups	chopped baby spinach
2 tbsp	nutritional yeast (optional)

TEST KITCHEN TIP

Nutritional yeast, a common ingredient in vegan recipes, adds a nutty, distinctly cheese-like flavour. Use it in sauces and gravies, or sprinkle it over scrambled eggs, salads, popcorn, pasta or potatoes.

Turkey Kielbasa Sweet Potato Skillet

MAKES 4 SERVINGS
HANDS-ON TIME 30 MINUTES
TOTAL TIME 30 MINUTES

1	large sweet potato (about 375 g), unpeeled
3 tbsp	canola oil, divided
250 g	turkey kielbasa sausage, casings removed and diced
1	sweet red pepper, diced
1 cup	jarred sauerkraut, including juices
4 cups	arugula or baby spinach
4	eggs
	salt (optional)
	pepper (optional)

Using fork, prick sweet potato all over; microwave on high until soft, 3 to 5 minutes. Let cool enough to handle. Chop into ¾-inch cubes.

In large nonstick skillet, heat 2 tbsp of the oil over medium-high heat. Cook sweet potatoes, stirring frequently, until lightly crisped, 4 to 6 minutes. Add kielbasa and red pepper; cook, stirring often, until red pepper is softened, about 5 minutes.

Stir in sauerkraut; cook until liquid is absorbed, about 1 minute. Stir in arugula until combined. Transfer to bowl; cover and keep warm.

Wipe pan clean. Add remaining 1 tbsp oil to pan; heat over medium-high heat. Cook eggs until whites are set but yolks are still runny, about 3 minutes. Sprinkle with salt and pepper (if using). Divide sweet potato mixture among serving plates; top each with egg.

NUTRITIONAL INFORMATION PER SERVING about 327 cal, 19 g pro, 21 g total fat (4 g sat. fat), 17 g carb (3 g dietary fibre, 5 g sugar), 225 mg chol, 874 mg sodium, 275 mg potassium. % RDI: 14% calcium, 17% iron, 180% vit A, 150% vit C, 9% folate.

TEST KITCHEN TIP

Use up leftover sauerkraut wherever you need a hit of tart flavour and crunch. It's great on a sausage in a bun or on burgers topped with sharp aged cheddar cheese.

Thai Peanut Beef Tacos

MAKES 10 TACOS
HANDS-ON TIME 15 MINUTES
TOTAL TIME 15 MINUTES

In large nonstick skillet, cook beef over medium-high heat, breaking up with spoon, until no longer pink, about 5 minutes. Add curry paste, peanut butter and water, stirring until combined. Remove from heat.

Place coleslaw in centre of each tortilla; top with beef mixture, mango and cilantro. Serve with peanuts and lime wedges (if using).

NUTRITIONAL INFORMATION PER TACO about 180 cal, 11 g pro, 9 g total fat (3 g sat. fat), 16 g carb (2 g dietary fibre, 4 g sugar), 27 mg chol, 172 mg sodium, 213 mg potassium. % RDI: 3% calcium, 9% iron, 17% vit A, 13% vit C, 6% folate.

450 g	lean ground beef
3 tbsp	Thai red curry paste (such as Thai Kitchen)
2 tbsp	smooth peanut butter
2 tbsp	water
10	small soft corn or flour tortillas
1½ cups	colourful coleslaw mix
1	mango, peeled, pitted and diced
¼ cup	packed fresh cilantro leaves, torn
	chopped peanuts (optional)
	lime wedges (optional)

TEST KITCHEN TIP

Feel free to use ground chicken, turkey or pork instead of beef in this recipe. To heat tortillas one at a time, place in a hot dry skillet for 15 seconds per side. When you're serving a large group, it's easier to fan the tortillas on a baking sheet and bake in a 400°F oven until warmed, 1 to 2 minutes.

Skillet Stroganoff Pie

MAKES 4 TO 6 SERVINGS
HANDS-ON TIME 25 MINUTES
TOTAL TIME 30 MINUTES

3	large russet potatoes (about 1 kg total)
450 g	extra-lean ground beef
2 tbsp	butter, divided
1	small onion, chopped
2	cloves garlic, minced
2 tsp	chopped fresh thyme
1	227 g pkg cremini or button mushrooms, sliced
1¼ tsp	salt, divided
¾ tsp	pepper, divided
1 tbsp	Dijon mustard
2 tsp	Worcestershire sauce
2 tbsp	all-purpose flour
1¼ cups	water
¾ cup	frozen peas
¼ cup	sour cream
1 cup	milk, warmed
2 tbsp	chopped fresh parsley

Using fork, prick potatoes all over. Microwave on high, turning once, until fork-tender, 8 to 10 minutes. Set aside until cool enough to handle.

Meanwhile, in 10-inch cast-iron or ovenproof skillet, cook beef over medium-high heat, breaking up with spoon, until no longer pink, about 4 minutes. Using slotted spoon, transfer beef to bowl. Set aside.

Drain fat from skillet. Add 1 tbsp of the butter; melt over medium-high heat. Cook onion, garlic and thyme, stirring, until onion is softened, about 4 minutes. Add mushrooms, ¾ tsp of the salt and ½ tsp of the pepper; cook, stirring, until mushrooms are softened, about 4 minutes.

Stir in beef, mustard and Worcestershire sauce. Sprinkle with flour; cook, stirring, for 1 minute. Stir in water; bring to boil, scraping up browned bits. Reduce heat and simmer until thickened, about 5 minutes. Stir in peas and sour cream; remove from heat. Set aside.

Peel potatoes; place potato flesh in bowl. Add milk, parsley and remaining ½ tsp salt and ¼ tsp pepper; using potato masher, mash until smooth. Dollop over beef mixture, spreading to edge; dot top with remaining 1 tbsp butter. Broil until golden, 3 to 4 minutes. Let stand for 5 minutes before serving.

NUTRITIONAL INFORMATION PER EACH OF 6 SERVINGS about 338 cal, 23 g pro, 12 g total fat (6 g sat. fat), 35 g carb (4 g dietary fibre, 6 g sugar), 58 mg chol, 651 mg sodium, 1,034 mg potassium. % RDI: 10% calcium, 25% iron, 12% vit A, 40% vit C, 20% folate.

Beef & Bok Choy Satay

MAKES 4 SERVINGS
HANDS-ON TIME 15 MINUTES
TOTAL TIME 15 MINUTES

In small saucepan, heat 2 tbsp of the oil over medium heat; cook onion, garlic, soy sauce, peanut butter, brown sugar and lemon juice, stirring, until smooth and thickened, about 3 minutes. Set aside.

Sprinkle beef with salt. In large nonstick skillet or wok, heat 1½ tsp of the remaining oil over medium high-heat; cook half of the beef and bok choy, stirring, until golden, about 3 minutes. Repeat with remaining 1½ tsp oil, beef and bok choy.

In large bowl, toss beef mixture with sauce to coat. Sprinkle with cilantro, peanuts, and chili pepper (if using).

NUTRITIONAL INFORMATION PER SERVING about 311 cal, 27 g pro, 20 g total fat (4 g sat. fat), 7 g carb (2 g dietary fibre, 3 g sugar), 48 mg chol, 392 mg sodium, 706 mg potassium. % RDI: 8% calcium, 20% iron, 34% vit A, 42% vit C, 22% folate.

3 tbsp	olive oil, divided
half	onion, minced
1	clove garlic, minced
1 tbsp	sodium-reduced soy sauce
2 tsp	smooth peanut butter
1 tsp	packed brown sugar
1 tsp	lemon juice
400 g	beef eye of round oven roast, cut in ¼-inch thick slices
¼ tsp	salt
2	heads Shanghai bok choy, cut in 1-inch chunks
⅓ cup	torn fresh cilantro
¼ cup	chopped unsalted peanuts
	sliced red finger chili pepper (optional)

TEST KITCHEN TIP

Shanghai bok choy is similar to regular bok choy, but has pale green stalks and a slightly sweeter flavour. Rinse bok choy thoroughly; like celery and leeks, the stalks can retain dirt and grit.

MAKES 4 SERVINGS

HANDS-ON TIME 25 MINUTES

TOTAL TIME 25 MINUTES

Steak & Asparagus Stir-Fry

½ cup	water, divided (approx)
2 tbsp	oyster sauce
1 tsp	chili garlic sauce
¼ tsp	each salt and pepper, divided
450 g	beef flank marinating steak, thinly sliced across the grain
4	cloves garlic, minced
1	egg yolk
2 tsp	cornstarch
1 tbsp	vegetable oil, divided
1	onion, thinly sliced
100 g	shiitake mushrooms, stemmed and sliced
1	bunch asparagus (about 450 g), trimmed and cut in 1½-inch lengths
1	sweet red pepper, thinly sliced

In small bowl, whisk together ⅓ cup water, the oyster sauce, chili garlic sauce and half each of the salt and pepper. Set aside.

In bowl, toss together beef, garlic, egg yolk, cornstarch and remaining salt and pepper. In large nonstick skillet or wok, heat 1 tsp of the oil over medium-high heat; stir-fry half of the beef mixture until browned, about 3 minutes. Transfer to plate. Repeat with 1 tsp of the remaining oil and the remaining beef mixture.

In same pan, heat remaining 1 tsp oil over medium-high heat; stir-fry onion and mushrooms until onion is golden and mushrooms are softened, about 4 minutes.

Add asparagus, red pepper and 2 tbsp of the remaining water; stir-fry until asparagus is tender-crisp, about 6 minutes. Return beef and any accumulated juices to pan. Stir in oyster sauce mixture; cook, stirring, until slightly thickened, about 1 minute.

NUTRITIONAL INFORMATION PER SERVING about 284 cal, 28 g pro, 14 g total fat (5 g sat. fat), 11 g carb (3 g dietary fibre, 3 g sugar), 101 mg chol, 476 mg sodium, 664 mg potassium. % RDI: 4% calcium, 22% iron, 17% vit A, 93% vit C, 20% folate.

TEST KITCHEN TIP

Coating thinly sliced beef with egg yolk and cornstarch, or "velveting," helps keep the meat tender by protecting it from the heat of your wok. Stir-frying the steak in two batches is also important; cooking it all at once will cause it to steam rather than fry, which can give it a rubbery texture.

Beef & Bean Chili

MAKES 8 SERVINGS
HANDS-ON TIME 10 MINUTES
COOKING TIME 6 HOURS
TOTAL TIME 6½ HOURS

In slow cooker, combine beef, garlic, celery, red onion, chili powder, oregano, cumin and salt; stir in tomatoes, kidney beans, baked beans and jalapeño peppers. Cover and cook on low until vegetables are tender, 6 to 8 hours.

Whisk flour with water until smooth; stir into slow cooker. Cover and cook on high until slightly thickened, 15 to 20 minutes. Serve topped with avocado, cheddar, sour cream, green onions, tostadas and cilantro (if using).

NUTRITIONAL INFORMATION PER SERVING about 246 cal, 32 g pro, 18 g total fat (7 g sat. fat), 39 g carb (10 g dietary fibre, 14 g sugar), 68 mg chol, 882 mg sodium, 1,161 mg potassium. % RDI: 17% calcium, 55% iron, 19% vit A, 77% vit C, 25% folate.

900 g	lean ground beef
5	cloves garlic, minced
3	ribs celery, thinly sliced
1	large red onion, diced
4 tbsp	chili powder
2 tbsp	each dried oregano and ground cumin
½ tsp	salt
2	796 ml cans whole plum tomatoes, crushed by hand
1	540 ml can red kidney beans, drained and rinsed
1	398 ml can baked beans in tomato sauce
½ cup	drained pickled sliced jalapeño peppers
2 tbsp	all-purpose flour
2 tbsp	water

TOPPINGS (OPTIONAL)

sliced pitted peeled avocado

shredded cheddar cheese

sour cream

sliced green onions

corn tostadas

fresh cilantro or parsley

TEST KITCHEN TIP

If you like your chili spicy with a little smoky flavour, mince two to three canned chipotle chilies in adobo sauce and add them when you stir in the jalapeños.

MAKES 8 SERVINGS
HANDS-ON TIME 15 MINUTES
COOKING TIME 7¼ HOURS
TOTAL TIME 7½ HOURS

Slow Cooker
Massaman Beef Curry

MASSAMAN CURRY PASTE

1 tbsp	coriander seeds
1 tsp	each cinnamon and ground cardamom
¼ tsp	ground cloves
3	shallots, halved lengthwise
1	stalk lemongrass, outer layers discarded and thinly sliced
6	cloves garlic
1	piece (1 inch) fresh ginger, peeled and thinly sliced
1	red finger chili pepper, seeded
¼ cup	water
2 tbsp	tomato paste
2 tbsp	fish sauce
1 tsp	packed brown sugar
½ tsp	salt

BEEF CURRY

900 g	beef stewing cubes, cut in 1-inch chunks
2	large white potatoes (about 450 g total), peeled and cut in 1-inch chunks
1	400 ml can coconut milk
2 tbsp	all-purpose flour
3 tbsp	water
1	red finger chili pepper, thinly sliced (optional)

MASSAMAN CURRY PASTE In dry small skillet, toast coriander seeds, cinnamon, cardamom and cloves over medium heat, shaking pan and stirring often, until fragrant, about 3 minutes.

In food processor, purée together coriander mixture, shallots, lemongrass, garlic, ginger, chili pepper, water, tomato paste, fish sauce, brown sugar and salt, scraping down side, until thick paste forms, about 3 minutes. *(Make-ahead: Refrigerate in airtight container for up to 24 hours.)*

BEEF CURRY In slow cooker, combine beef, potatoes, coconut milk and curry paste. Cover and cook on low until beef is tender, 7 to 8 hours.

Whisk flour with water until smooth; stir into slow cooker. Cover and cook on high until thickened, about 15 minutes. Sprinkle with chili pepper (if using).

NUTRITIONAL INFORMATION PER SERVING about 332 cal, 27 g pro, 18 g total fat (12 g sat. fat), 16 g carb (2 g dietary fibre, 3 g sugar), 61 mg chol, 579 mg sodium, 728 mg potassium. % RDI: 4% calcium, 34% iron, 2% vit A, 12% vit C, 10% folate.

TEST KITCHEN TIP

When you're prepping hot chilies, wear disposable gloves—the natural chemical that makes chilies spicy, capsaicin, can persist on your hands and get in your eyes if you inadvertently rub them later. In most chilies, capsaicin is concentrated in the white veins and the seeds. If you prefer less heat, seed and devein the chili. Using a small spoon, scoop out the seeds, then trim away the veins with a paring knife.

Slow Cooker Beef & Barley Pot Roast

MAKES 8 TO 10 SERVINGS
HANDS-ON TIME 10 MINUTES
COOKING TIME 6 HOURS
TOTAL TIME 6¼ HOURS

Combine garlic, ½ tsp of the salt, the pepper and thyme; rub all over beef. Place in slow cooker. Add onions, carrots, mushrooms, barley and bay leaf.

Whisk together broth, water, tomato paste, soy sauce and remaining ¼ tsp salt; pour into slow cooker. Cover and cook on low until beef is tender, 6 to 8 hours.

Transfer beef to cutting board; tent with foil and let rest for 10 minutes before slicing. Skim fat from cooking liquid; discard bay leaf. Stir Worcestershire sauce into slow cooker. Over large bowl, strain barley mixture to make gravy, reserving barley. Serve barley mixture and gravy with beef.

NUTRITIONAL INFORMATION PER EACH OF 10 SERVINGS about 280 cal, 28 g pro, 14 g total fat (6 g sat. fat), 10 g carb (3 g dietary fibre, 2 g sugar), 78 mg chol, 445 mg sodium, 449 mg potassium. % RDI: 4% calcium, 24% iron, 27% vit A, 3% vit C, 6% folate.

3	cloves garlic, minced
¾ tsp	salt, divided
½ tsp	each pepper and dried thyme
1.35 kg	boneless beef pot roast (top or bottom blade, or cross rib)
2	onions, sliced
2	carrots, coarsely chopped
1	216 g pkg cremini mushrooms, quartered
⅓ cup	pot or pearl barley
1	bay leaf
1½ cups	sodium-reduced beef broth
1 cup	water
1 tbsp	tomato paste
1 tbsp	sodium-reduced soy sauce
1 tbsp	Worcestershire sauce

TEST KITCHEN TIP

Pot barley is whole grain barley that has only the outer, inedible hull removed. It takes longer to cook than the polished pearl barley, but it's more nutritious because it still has its bran and germ intact.

MAKES 6 TO 8 SERVINGS
HANDS-ON TIME 20 MINUTES
REFRIGERATING TIME 4 HOURS
TOTAL TIME 4½ HOURS

Grilled Flank Steak & Pebre Sauce

2	green onions, chopped
2	jalapeño peppers, seeded
1 cup	packed fresh cilantro
1 cup	packed fresh parsley
½ cup	water
¼ cup	olive oil
¼ cup	sherry vinegar or red wine vinegar
2	cloves garlic, minced
¼ tsp	salt
900 g	beef flank marinating steak
2	tomatoes, finely diced

In food processor, combine green onions, jalapeño peppers, cilantro, parsley and water. Pulse until finely chopped. Transfer to bowl. Stir in oil, vinegar, garlic and salt. Place steak in large dish; spoon half of the pebre sauce over steak, turning to coat. Cover and refrigerate steak and remaining sauce separately for 4 hours or overnight.

Reserving marinade, place steak on greased grill over medium-high heat; close lid and grill, turning once and basting with remaining marinade halfway through, until desired doneness, 8 to 10 minutes for medium-rare. Transfer to cutting board; let rest for 2 to 3 minutes before slicing thinly across the grain.

Meanwhile, stir tomatoes into reserved pebre sauce; serve with steak.

NUTRITIONAL INFORMATION PER EACH OF 8 SERVINGS about 262 cal, 26 g pro, 16 g total fat (4 g sat. fat), 3 g carb (1 g dietary fibre), 44 mg chol, 135 mg sodium. % RDI: 2% calcium, 17% iron, 9% vit A, 37% vit C, 11% folate.

MAKE IT A MEAL

Grilled Flank Steak & Pebre Sauce	262 cal
Add: 6 spears grilled asparagus	18 cal
1 cup grilled cherry tomatoes	27 cal
Total	**307 cal**

Orange Ginger Steak Salad

MAKES 6 SERVINGS
HANDS-ON TIME 15 MINUTES
TOTAL TIME 30 MINUTES

Position racks in top and bottom thirds of oven; preheat broiler to high. Place large baking sheet on bottom rack to heat. Pat steak dry with paper towel; season both sides with ½ tsp of the salt and the pepper.

In large bowl, whisk together peanut butter, chili paste, ginger, honey and remaining ½ tsp salt; whisk in vinegar and orange juice. Add broccoli slaw and kale; toss to combine.

Using tongs, transfer steak to prepared pan; broil on top rack, turning once, for 8 minutes. Remove from oven; transfer to cutting board. Tent with foil; let rest for 5 minutes.

Drizzle salad mixture with pan juices; toss to combine. Divide salad mixture among plates. Slice steak across the grain; garnish with broccoli sprouts (if using). Serve alongside salad.

NUTRITIONAL INFORMATION PER SERVING about 273 cal, 31 g pro, 13 g total fat (5 g sat. fat), 9 g carb (2 g dietary fibre, 4 g sugar), 59 mg chol, 521 mg sodium, 587 mg potassium. % RDI: 7% calcium, 24% iron, 36% vit A, 135% vit C, 40% folate.

750 g	beef flank marinating steak
1 tsp	salt, divided
½ tsp	pepper
2 tbsp	natural peanut butter
2 tsp	Asian chili paste (such as sambal oelek)
1 tsp	grated fresh ginger
1 tsp	liquid honey
¼ cup	rice vinegar
3 tbsp	orange juice
1	340 g pkg broccoli slaw
1	142 g pkg baby kale
	fresh broccoli sprouts (optional)

TEST KITCHEN TIP

Flavourful flank steak is a large thin cut that has a distinct grain; before serving, it's usually cut across the grain into thin, tender slices.

Beef

MAKES 4 SERVINGS
HANDS-ON TIME 25 MINUTES
TOTAL TIME 30 MINUTES

Bacon-Wrapped Beef Kabobs

4	strips bacon, halved lengthwise and cut crosswise in thirds
400 g	top sirloin grilling steak, cut in 1½-inch chunks
1	small sweet red pepper, cut in 1-inch pieces
half	red onion, cut in 1-inch pieces
8	large cremini mushrooms, stemmed and halved
2 tbsp	olive oil
1 tbsp	chopped fresh rosemary
1	clove garlic, minced
¼ tsp	each salt and pepper

Wrap 1 piece of bacon around each piece of steak, overlapping edges of bacon slightly. Alternately thread steak, red pepper, red onion and mushrooms onto metal or soaked wooden skewers, piercing both ends of each piece of bacon to secure.

Stir together oil, rosemary and garlic; brush onto skewers. Sprinkle with salt and pepper. Place on grill over medium-high heat; close lid and grill, turning occasionally, until steak is medium-rare, about 6 minutes. Let rest for 2 minutes before serving.

NUTRITIONAL INFORMATION PER SERVING about 259 cal, 24 g pro, 14 g total fat (4 g sat. fat), 8 g carb (2 g dietary fibre, 4 g sugar), 55 mg chol, 371 mg sodium, 595 mg potassium. % RDI: 2% calcium, 18% iron, 9% vit A, 82% vit C, 9% folate.

MAKE IT A MEAL

Bacon-Wrapped Beef Kabobs	259 cal
Add: Arugula & Mushroom Salad (page 139)	59 cal
6 stalks grilled asparagus	18 cal
Total	**336 cal**

Tamarind Flank Steak Noodle Bowl

MAKES 6 SERVINGS
HANDS-ON TIME 30 MINUTES
TOTAL TIME 30 MINUTES

In bowl, combine hot water with tamarind pulp; let stand until tamarind is softened, about 20 minutes.

Meanwhile, cook noodles according to package directions; drain. Set aside.

Meanwhile, in small bowl, whisk together water, fish sauce, lime juice, honey and chili sauce. Set aside.

Drain tamarind mixture, reserving ¼ cup of the liquid. In food processor, purée tamarind pulp with reserved liquid until smooth. Set aside. *(Make-ahead: Refrigerate in airtight container for up to 2 weeks.)*

Sprinkle beef with salt. In large nonstick skillet or wok, heat oil over high heat; stir-fry beef until browned all over, about 3 minutes. Using slotted spoon, transfer beef to bowl. Set aside.

In same skillet, stir-fry onion over high heat until golden, about 2 minutes. Add garlic; stir-fry until fragrant, about 1 minute. Add noodles, snow peas, fish sauce mixture and ¼ cup of the tamarind sauce; stir-fry until noodles are warmed through, about 3 minutes. Add beef and bean sprouts; stir-fry until sprouts are tender-crisp, about 1 minute. Reserve remaining sauce for another use.

NUTRITIONAL INFORMATION PER SERVING about 295 cal, 15 g pro, 6 g total fat (2 g sat. fat), 46 g carb (3 g dietary fibre, 14 g sugar), 24 mg chol, 536 mg sodium, 422 mg potassium. % RDI: 4% calcium, 17% iron, 2% vit A, 28% vit C, 18% folate.

⅔ cup	hot water
¼ cup	tamarind pulp
200 g	rice stick noodles (¼ inch wide)
¼ cup	water
2 tbsp	each fish sauce and lime juice
4 tsp	liquid honey
1 tsp	Asian chili sauce (such as sriracha)
300 g	beef flank marinating steak, thinly sliced across the grain
pinch	salt
2 tsp	vegetable oil
1	onion, thinly sliced
3	cloves garlic, finely chopped
2 cups	snow peas, trimmed
3 cups	bean sprouts

TEST KITCHEN TIP

Tamarind pulp has a tart, fruity flavour and is commonly used in Asian, South American and Middle Eastern cooking.

MAKES 4 SERVINGS
HANDS-ON TIME 30 MINUTES
TOTAL TIME 30 MINUTES

Steak & Egg Cobb Salad

COBB SALAD

2	eggs
1	beef strip loin grilling steak (about 400 g)
1½ **tsp**	canola oil
½ **tsp**	each salt and pepper
4 **cups**	baby arugula
4 **cups**	pea shoots
quarter	small red onion, thinly sliced
1	avocado, sliced
16	cherry tomatoes, halved
½ **cup**	crumbled feta cheese

BUTTERMILK HORSERADISH DRESSING

½ **cup**	buttermilk
¼ **cup**	sour cream
2 **tbsp**	white wine vinegar
2 **tbsp**	finely chopped chives
4 **tsp**	prepared horseradish
¼ **tsp**	each salt and pepper

COBB SALAD Fill small saucepan with water; bring to boil over high heat. Add eggs; cook for 7 minutes. Drain and rinse under cold water until chilled, about 2 minutes; drain again. Peel off shells; cut eggs into quarters.

Meanwhile, rub steak with oil, salt and pepper. In cast-iron skillet, cook over medium-high heat, flipping once, until medium-rare, 3 to 4 minutes per side. Transfer to cutting board; tent with foil and let rest for 5 minutes before thinly slicing across the grain.

Meanwhile, on large platter, combine arugula with pea shoots. Arrange red onion, avocado, tomatoes, eggs and steak over top. Sprinkle with feta.

BUTTERMILK HORSERADISH DRESSING In medium bowl, whisk together buttermilk, sour cream and vinegar; whisk in chives, horseradish, salt and pepper until combined. Drizzle ½ cup of the dressing over salad. Serve remaining dressing with salad, if desired, or reserve for another use.

NUTRITIONAL INFORMATION PER SERVING about 373 cal, 29 g pro, 25 g total fat (9 g sat. fat), 10 g carb (4 g dietary fibre, 4 g sugar), 163 mg chol, 627 mg sodium, 688 mg potassium. % RDI: 14% calcium, 22% iron, 23% vit A, 42% vit C, 45% folate.

TEST KITCHEN TIP

You may not need all of the dressing for this salad. If you don't use it all, you can drizzle the extra over potato salad, or serve it as a dip for crudités or chicken wings.

Vegetable Beef Noodle Soup

MAKES 6 SERVINGS
HANDS-ON TIME 20 MINUTES
TOTAL TIME 2½ HOURS

Sprinkle beef with pepper and salt. In Dutch oven or large heavy-bottomed pot, heat oil over medium-high heat; cook beef, stirring occasionally, until browned, about 6 minutes. Stir in carrots, celery, onion and garlic; cook, stirring occasionally, until vegetables are softened, about 6 minutes.

Stir in broth, water, tomato paste, herbes de Provence and vinegar. Bring to boil; reduce heat and simmer, stirring occasionally, until beef is tender, about 2 hours.

Stir in noodles and peas; cook over medium heat until noodles are tender, about 5 minutes. Stir in spinach.

NUTRITIONAL INFORMATION PER SERVING about 226 cal, 20 g pro, 10 g total fat (3 g sat. fat), 14 g carb (3 g dietary fibre, 4 g sugar), 50 mg chol, 593 mg sodium, 519 mg potassium. % RDI: 7% calcium, 20% iron, 83% vit A, 12% vit C, 20% folate.

MAKE IT A MEAL

Vegetable Beef Noodle Soup	226 cal
Add: 1 crusty roll	167 cal
Total	**393 cal**

450 g	beef stewing cubes
½ tsp	pepper
¼ tsp	salt
1 tbsp	vegetable oil
3	carrots, chopped
2	ribs celery, chopped
1	onion, chopped
3	cloves garlic, minced
1	900 ml pkg sodium-reduced beef broth
3 cups	water
2 tbsp	tomato paste
1 tsp	herbes de Provence
½ tsp	red wine vinegar
1 cup	large curly egg noodles
½ cup	frozen peas
3 cups	baby spinach

Slow Cooker
Beef & Lemongrass Noodle Soup

MAKES 8 SERVINGS
HANDS-ON TIME 20 MINUTES
COOKING TIME 8¼ HOURS
TOTAL TIME 8¼ HOURS

4 cups	water
3 cups	sodium-reduced beef broth
6	slices (½ inch thick) fresh ginger
2	stalks lemongrass, trimmed, halved crosswise and bruised with back of knife
2	star anise
¾ tsp	salt
800 g	boneless beef blade pot roast, trimmed
3	200 g pkgs fresh udon noodles
1 cup	julienned carrots
1 tbsp	fish sauce
1 tbsp	lime juice
½ cup	fresh cilantro leaves, torn and divided

In slow cooker, combine water, broth, ginger, lemongrass, star anise and salt. Add beef, pushing to submerge; cover and cook on low until beef is tender, about 8 hours.

Using slotted spoon, transfer beef to cutting board. Set aside.

Discard ginger, lemongrass and star anise. Skim fat from surface of cooking liquid. Stir noodles and carrots into slow cooker; cover and cook on high until tender, about 10 minutes.

Meanwhile, using 2 forks, shred beef, discarding any fat. When noodles are tender, stir in beef, fish sauce, lime juice and ¼ cup of the cilantro. Ladle soup into serving bowls; sprinkle with remaining ¼ cup cilantro.

NUTRITIONAL INFORMATION PER SERVING about 239 cal, 25 g pro, 4 g total fat (1 g sat. fat), 24 g carb (1 g dietary fibre, 1 g sugar), 55 mg chol, 852 mg sodium, 342 mg potassium. % RDI: 3% calcium, 18% iron, 17% vit A, 2% vit C, 3% folate.

Lamb Chops
With Mint Gremolata & Mini Potatoes

MAKES 4 SERVINGS
HANDS-ON TIME 25 MINUTES
TOTAL TIME 25 MINUTES

MINI POTATOES In large pot of boiling salted water, cook potatoes until tender, about 15 minutes; drain. Transfer to bowl; toss with lemon zest, oil, salt and pepper.

MINT GREMOLATA Meanwhile, in small bowl, whisk together garlic, mint, oil, lemon zest, salt and pepper; set aside.

Rub lamb chops with oil; sprinkle with salt and pepper. In large skillet over medium heat, cook lamb chops until desired doneness, about 8 minutes for medium-rare. Top lamb with gremolata; serve with potatoes.

NUTRITIONAL INFORMATION PER SERVING about 290 cal, 14 g pro, 14 g total fat (3 g sat. fat), 29 g carb (3 g dietary fibre, 1 g sugar), 26 mg chol, 382 mg sodium, 692 mg potassium. %RDI: 32% calcium, 16% iron, 1% vit A, 35% vit C, 11% folate.

MAKE IT A MEAL

Lamb Chops With Mint Gremolata & Mini Potatoes	290 cal
Add: Creamy Cucumber Salad (page 141)	38 cal
Total	**328 cal**

MINI POTATOES

1	680 g bag yellow-fleshed mini potatoes
1 tsp	grated lemon zest
1 tsp	olive oil
pinch	each salt and pepper

MINT GREMOLATA

2	cloves garlic, minced
2 tbsp	finely chopped fresh mint
2 tbsp	olive oil
1 tbsp	grated lemon zest
pinch	each salt and pepper
8	frenched lamb chops (about 450 g total), trimmed
1 tsp	olive oil
pinch	each salt and pepper

Herbed Lamb Chops & Grilled Vegetables

MAKES 4 SERVINGS
HANDS-ON TIME 20 MINUTES
TOTAL TIME 50 MINUTES

¼ **cup**	white balsamic vinegar
¼ **cup**	olive oil
4	cloves garlic, minced
3 **tbsp**	finely chopped fresh rosemary
1 **tbsp**	each chopped fresh thyme, sage and parsley
½ **tsp**	each salt and pepper
8	lamb loin chops, trimmed (about 750 g total)
450 g	asparagus, trimmed
2	sweet red or yellow peppers, seeded, cored and each cut into 8 wedges
½ **cup**	crumbled feta cheese

In shallow glass dish, stir together vinegar, oil, garlic, rosemary, thyme, sage, parsley, salt and pepper. Transfer 3 tbsp of mixture to separate shallow glass dish and set aside for vegetables. Add lamb to remaining marinade, turning to coat. Cover and refrigerate for 30 minutes. *(Make-ahead: Refrigerate for up to 4 hours.)*

Discarding marinade, place chops on greased grill over medium-high heat. Close lid and grill, turning once, until desired doneness, about 4 minutes per side for medium-rare. Transfer to plate; tent with foil and let rest for 5 minutes.

Meanwhile, toss asparagus and peppers in reserved 3 tbsp marinade. Place vegetables on greased grill over medium-high heat; close lid and grill, turning once, until tender-crisp, about 8 minutes.

Transfer vegetables to platter; top with lamb chops. Sprinkle with feta.

NUTRITIONAL INFORMATION PER SERVING about 298 cal, 23 g pro, 19 g total fat (6 g sat. fat), 12 g carb (3 g dietary fibre), 86 mg chol, 447 mg sodium. % RDI: 13% calcium, 20% iron, 33% vit A, 177% vit C, 61% folate.

TEST KITCHEN TIP

If you don't have white balsamic vinegar on hand, you can replace it with ¼ cup white wine vinegar combined with 1 tsp granulated sugar.

Grilled Lamb Shoulder Chops
With Tomato Lentil Salad

MAKES 4 SERVINGS
HANDS-ON TIME 15 MINUTES
TOTAL TIME 20 MINUTES

TOMATO LENTIL SALAD   Drain and rinse lentils. In large bowl, toss together lentils, tomatoes, parsley, vinegars and oil; set aside.

GRILLED LAMB SHOULDER CHOPS   In small bowl, mix together garlic, rosemary, pepper and salt; rub all over chops. Place on greased grill over medium-high heat; close lid and grill, turning once, until desired doneness, about 4 minutes per side for medium-rare. Serve with Tomato Lentil Salad and lemon wedges.

NUTRITIONAL INFORMATION PER SERVING about 277 cal, 27 g pro, 9 g total fat (3 g sat. fat), 23 g carb, 68 mg chol, 562 mg sodium. % RDI: 4% calcium, 38% iron, 4% vit A, 18% vit C, 86% folate.

TOMATO LENTIL SALAD

1	540 ml can lentils
½ cup	chopped tomato
¼ cup	chopped fresh parsley
2 tbsp	sherry vinegar or wine vinegar
1 tbsp	extra-virgin olive oil

GRILLED LAMB SHOULDER CHOPS

3	cloves garlic, minced
1 tbsp	chopped fresh rosemary (or 1 tsp dried)
1 tsp	coarsely ground pepper
½ tsp	salt
4	lamb shoulder chops (about 750 g total)
	lemon wedges

TEST KITCHEN TIP

If you prefer, use lamb loin chops instead of shoulder chops. Lamb shoulder chops, a less-expensive cut, have a slightly chewier texture and a more steak-like flavour than loin chops.

North African Pork Chops
With Cauliflower Couscous

MAKES 4 SERVINGS
HANDS-ON TIME 15 MINUTES
TOTAL TIME 15 MINUTES

1	small head cauliflower, cut in florets (approximately 7 cups)
2½ tsp	olive oil, divided
½ tsp	each salt and pepper, divided
½ cup	chopped fresh cilantro, divided
4	boneless pork loin chops (about 450 g total)
1 tbsp	ras el hanout, divided
1	796 ml can diced tomatoes
3 tbsp	tomato paste
¼ tsp	onion powder
¼ tsp	garlic powder

Preheat oven to 400°F. In food processor, pulse cauliflower into rice-size pieces. Spread onto parchment paper–lined baking sheet; drizzle with ½ tsp of the oil and sprinkle with ¼ tsp each of the salt and pepper. Toss to coat. Bake, stirring once, until dry, about 10 minutes. Stir in ¼ cup of the cilantro.

Meanwhile, sprinkle pork with remaining ¼ tsp each salt and pepper; rub all over with 1½ tsp of the ras el hanout. In large nonstick skillet, heat remaining 2 tsp oil over medium-high heat; cook pork, turning once, until instant-read thermometer inserted sideways in centre reads 155°F, 6 to 8 minutes. Transfer to plate; keep warm.

In same pan, bring tomatoes, tomato paste, onion powder, garlic powder and remaining 1½ tsp ras el hanout to boil over medium-high heat; cook, stirring, until thickened, about 4 minutes. Stir in remaining ¼ cup cilantro. Add pork chops and any accumulated juices; cook until heated through. Serve over cauliflower mixture.

NUTRITIONAL INFORMATION PER SERVING about 324 cal, 31 g pro, 14 g total fat (5 g sat. fat), 20 g carb (9 g dietary fibre, 10 g sugar), 61 mg chol, 711 mg sodium, 1,233 mg potassium. % RDI: 12% calcium, 29% iron, 9% vit A, 210% vit C, 52% folate.

TEST KITCHEN TIP

Ras el hanout is a North African spice blend, available in Middle Eastern grocery stores and specialty spice shops. Some blends have up to 50 ingredients, but here's a simpler version: Mix ½ tsp each ground cumin, ground ginger, turmeric and salt; ¼ tsp each granulated sugar and pepper; and pinch each cayenne pepper, cinnamon, ground allspice, ground fennel seeds and ground cloves.

Quick Thai Pork Stir-Fry

MAKES 4 TO 6 SERVINGS
HANDS-ON TIME 20 MINUTES
TOTAL TIME 20 MINUTES

In nonstick skillet or wok, heat oil over medium-high heat. Cook pork, breaking up with spoon, until no longer pink, 3 to 4 minutes.

Stir in garlic; cook for 1 minute. Stir in fish sauce and chili paste; cook for 2 minutes.

Stir in oyster sauce, water and honey; add bok choy and red pepper. Stir-fry until bok choy starts to wilt, about 2 minutes. Remove from heat; stir in basil. Sprinkle with chopped peanuts (if using).

NUTRITIONAL INFORMATION PER EACH OF 6 SERVINGS about 193 cal, 15 g pro, 12 g total fat (4 g sat. fat), 5 g carb (1 g dietary fibre, 3 g sugar), 47 mg chol, 558 mg sodium, 428 mg potassium. % RDI: 6% calcium, 11% iron, 27% vit A, 75% vit C, 12% folate.

1 tsp	vegetable oil
425 g	lean ground pork
3	cloves garlic, minced
1 tbsp	fish sauce
1 tbsp	Asian chili paste (such as sambal oelek)
3 tbsp	oyster sauce
2 tbsp	water
1 tsp	liquid honey
4	heads baby bok choy, thinly sliced (about 4 cups total)
1	sweet red pepper, thinly sliced
¼ cup	chopped fresh basil
	chopped peanuts or chopped cashews (optional)

TEST KITCHEN TIP

Serve this dish over rice vermicelli, prepared according to package directions.
To make a heartier meal, top each serving with a fried egg.

Jerk-Spiced Pork Chops
With Rice, Peppers and Green Peas

MAKES 4 SERVINGS
HANDS-ON TIME 15 MINUTES
TOTAL TIME 30 MINUTES

2 tbsp	olive oil, divided
1 tbsp	each soy sauce and orange juice
2	cloves garlic, minced
3	green onions, minced
1 tsp	each allspice and dried thyme
½ tsp	each salt and pepper, divided
¼ tsp	ground ginger
pinch	cayenne pepper
4	pork loin centre chops
1	small onion, chopped
1	sweet red pepper, chopped
¾ cup	parboiled rice
1½ cups	chicken broth
¼ tsp	cinnamon
¾ cup	frozen peas

Preheat oven to 375°F. In shallow dish, combine 1 tbsp of the oil and the soy sauce, orange juice, garlic, green onions, allspice, thyme, ¼ tsp each of the salt and pepper, the ginger and cayenne. Add pork chops and rub mixture on both sides. Set aside.

In saucepan, heat remaining 1 tbsp oil over medium-high heat; cook onion, stirring occasionally, until softened, about 3 minutes. Add red pepper and rice; stir for 1 minute.

Add broth, cinnamon, and remaining ¼ tsp each salt and pepper; bring to boil. Reduce heat, cover and simmer until rice is tender and liquid is absorbed, about 20 minutes. Using fork, stir in peas; heat through.

Meanwhile, transfer pork to small roasting pan. Bake until instant-read thermometer inserted sideways in centre reads 155°F, about 18 minutes. Serve over rice and vegetables.

NUTRITIONAL INFORMATION PER SERVING about 397 cal, 27 g pro, 14 g total fat (4 g sat. fat), 38 g carb (3 g dietary fibre), 58 mg chol, 913 mg sodium. % RDI: 7% calcium, 17% iron, 12% vit A, 94% vit C, 12% folate.

TEST KITCHEN TIP

To keep spices as fresh and flavourful as possible, store in airtight containers, away from light, heat and humidity. Spices lose flavour over time, so replace them after about 6 months.

Seared Mustard Pork Chops
With Sautéed Red Cabbage

MAKES 4 SERVINGS
HANDS-ON TIME 30 MINUTES
TOTAL TIME 30 MINUTES

In large nonstick skillet, heat 2 tsp of the oil over medium-high heat; cook onion, stirring frequently, until softened, about 8 minutes. Push to side of pan.

Add cabbage to pan; cook, stirring occasionally, until beginning to soften, about 5 minutes. Stir in water, salt and pepper; cook until cabbage is softened, about 5 minutes. Transfer to platter and keep warm.

Sprinkle pinch each salt and pepper over both sides of chops. In same pan, heat remaining 2 tsp oil over medium-high heat; brown pork chops on both sides, turning once, about 5 minutes. Remove and set aside.

Add wine, mustard, and pinch each salt and pepper to pan, scraping up browned bits. Return chops to pan; cook until instant-read thermometer inserted sideways in centre reads 155°F, about 2 minutes.

Place chops on cabbage; drizzle with sauce.

4 tsp	olive oil, divided
1	sweet onion (such as Vidalia), thinly sliced
6 cups	sliced red cabbage
¼ cup	water
¼ tsp	each salt and pepper
4	bone-in pork chops (about 565 g total)
½ cup	dry white wine
1 tbsp	grainy Dijon mustard

NUTRITIONAL INFORMATION PER SERVING about 306 cal, 26 g pro, 15 g total fat (4 g sat. fat), 14 g carb (4 g dietary fibre, 8 g sugar), 77 mg chol, 272 mg sodium, 778 mg potassium. % RDI: 8% calcium, 13% iron, 1% vit A, 23% vit C, 18% folate.

MAKE IT A MEAL

Seared Mustard Pork Chops With Sautéed Red Cabbage	306 cal
Add: 1 cup steamed rapini	44 cal
Total	**350 cal**

MAKES 4 TO 6 SERVINGS
HANDS-ON TIME 20 MINUTES
TOTAL TIME 20 MINUTES

Sausage Choucroute Garnie

2	yellow-fleshed potatoes
1 tbsp	olive oil, divided
200 g	kielbasa sausage, halved lengthwise and cut in ½-inch thick slices
1	onion, sliced
1	750 ml jar sauerkraut, drained
2	whole cloves
1	bay leaf
¼ tsp	ground allspice
¼ tsp	pepper
pinch	salt
1 cup	Riesling or other white wine
1	Gala apple, cored and chopped
2 tsp	grainy mustard
2 tbsp	chopped fresh parsley

Using fork, prick potatoes all over. Microwave on high, turning once, until fork-tender, 6 to 8 minutes. Let cool enough to handle. Peel potatoes; coarsely chop potato flesh.

While potatoes are cooking, in Dutch oven or large heavy-bottomed pot, heat 1½ tsp of the oil over medium-high heat; cook sausage, stirring occasionally, until browned all over, about 2 minutes. Scrape into bowl. Set aside.

In same pot, heat remaining 1½ tsp oil over medium heat; cook onion, stirring often, until softened, about 5 minutes. Add sauerkraut, cloves, bay leaf, allspice, pepper and salt; cook, stirring, until fragrant, about 30 seconds.

Stir in sausage and wine; bring to boil. Reduce heat and simmer, stirring occasionally, until almost no liquid remains, 8 to 10 minutes. Add potatoes, apple and mustard; cook, stirring occasionally, until apple is warmed through, about 2 minutes. Discard cloves and bay leaf. Stir in parsley.

NUTRITIONAL INFORMATION PER EACH OF 6 SERVINGS about 192 cal, 9 g pro, 6 g total fat (2 g sat. fat), 22 g carb (4 g dietary fibre, 7 g sugar), 21 mg chol, 899 mg sodium, 545 mg potassium. % RDI: 5% calcium, 13% iron, 1% vit A, 33% vit C, 13% folate.

Quick Cassoulet Stew

MAKES 6 SERVINGS
HANDS-ON TIME 25 MINUTES
TOTAL TIME 30 MINUTES

In Dutch oven or large heavy-bottomed pot, heat 1½ tsp of the oil over medium heat; cook onion, fennel, carrots, garlic, thyme and rosemary, stirring often, until beginning to soften, about 5 minutes. Using slotted spoon, transfer to plate. Set aside.

Sprinkle chicken with salt. Add remaining 1½ tsp oil to pan; heat over medium-high heat. Cook chicken and sausage, stirring occasionally, until no longer pink inside, about 4 minutes. Sprinkle with flour; cook, stirring, for 1 minute.

Stir in onion mixture, tomatoes, beans and water, scraping up browned bits; bring to boil. Reduce heat, cover and simmer, stirring occasionally, until slightly thickened and vegetables are tender, 5 to 7 minutes. Discard thyme.

While stew is simmering, in skillet, melt butter over medium heat; cook bread crumbs, stirring often, until golden brown, about 5 minutes. Stir in 1 tbsp of the parsley.

Stir remaining parsley into stew. Sprinkle with bread crumb mixture.

NUTRITIONAL INFORMATION PER SERVING about 297 cal, 19 g pro, 13 g total fat (4 g sat. fat), 28 g carb (8 g dietary fibre, 8 g sugar), 55 mg chol, 589 mg sodium, 751 mg potassium. % RDI: 11% calcium, 25% iron, 48% vit A, 43% vit C, 20% folate.

1 tbsp	olive oil, divided
1	onion, chopped
half	bulb fennel, trimmed, cored and coarsely chopped
2	carrots, coarsely chopped
4	cloves garlic, minced
3	sprigs fresh thyme
1 tsp	minced fresh rosemary
4	boneless skinless chicken thighs (about 285 g total), cut in bite-size pieces
pinch	salt
1 cup	thinly sliced smoked farmer's sausage
1 tbsp	all-purpose flour
1	796 ml can diced tomatoes
1	540 ml can white kidney beans, drained and rinsed
1 cup	water
2 tsp	butter
½ cup	fresh bread crumbs
¼ cup	chopped fresh parsley, divided

TEST KITCHEN TIP

Make fresh bread crumbs by pulsing cubed day-old bread in a food processor until in fine crumbs. To store leftover fresh bread crumbs, place in a resealable freezer bag, pressing out as much air as possible, and freeze for up to four weeks.

MAKES 6 SERVINGS
HANDS-ON TIME 15 MINUTES
TOTAL TIME 15 MINUTES

Mediterranean Chickpea Stew

3	strips bacon, chopped
1	onion, chopped
1	227 g pkg cremini mushrooms, cut in quarters
2	ribs celery, chopped
2	cloves garlic, finely grated or pressed
1 tbsp	tomato paste
2 tsp	dried savory
¼ tsp	dried fennel seeds, crushed
1	796 ml can whole tomatoes, crushed by hand
2 cups	sodium-reduced chicken broth
1	540 ml can chickpeas, drained and rinsed
½ tsp	each salt and pepper
4 cups	baby spinach
1 tbsp	lemon juice
¼ cup	2% yogurt

In Dutch oven or large heavy-bottomed pot, cook bacon over medium heat, stirring often, until crisp, about 4 minutes. Using slotted spoon, transfer to paper towel–lined plate to drain. Set aside.

Drain all but 1 tbsp fat from pot; cook onion, mushrooms and celery over medium heat, stirring, until softened, about 5 minutes. Add garlic, tomato paste, savory and fennel seeds; cook, stirring, for 1 minute. Add tomatoes and broth; bring to boil. Reduce heat and simmer for 2 minutes. Stir in chickpeas, salt and pepper; cook until heated through. Remove from heat; stir in spinach and lemon juice.

Divide stew among serving bowls; dollop with yogurt. Sprinkle with bacon.

NUTRITIONAL INFORMATION PER SERVING about 189 cal, 11 g pro, 6 g total fat (2 g sat. fat), 26 g carb (7 g dietary fibre, 9 g sugar), 9 mg chol, 844 mg sodium, 784 mg potassium. % RDI: 14% calcium, 24% iron, 31% vit A, 42% vit C, 36% folate.

MAKE IT A MEAL

Mediterranean Chickpea Stew	189 cal
Add: 1 piece baguette (3 inch)	145 cal
Total	**334 cal**

Lemongrass Pork Tenderloin
With Honeyed Carrots & Beans

MAKES 4 SERVINGS
HANDS-ON TIME 30 MINUTES
REFRIGERATION TIME 8 HOURS
TOTAL TIME 8½ HOURS

LEMONGRASS PORK TENDERLOIN Add pork to large shallow dish. Whisk together 3 tbsp of the oil, the lime zest, lime juice, ginger, lemongrass, garlic and honey; pour over pork, rubbing all over. Cover and refrigerate for 8 hours. *(Make-ahead: Refrigerate for up to 24 hours.)* Remove pork from marinade, brushing off excess; discard marinade.

Preheat oven to 400°F. Sprinkle pork with salt and pepper. In nonstick skillet, heat remaining 1 tbsp oil over medium-high heat; cook pork, turning, until browned, about 6 minutes.

Transfer to foil-lined baking sheet. Bake until just a hint of pink remains inside or instant-read thermometer inserted sideways in centre reads 155°F, about 15 minutes. Transfer pork to cutting board; tent with foil. Let rest for 5 minutes before slicing. Transfer to serving dish. Sprinkle with cilantro.

HONEYED CARROTS & BEANS While pork is cooking, in large pot of boiling water, cook carrots just until tender, about 4 minutes. Add green beans and cook until tender-crisp, about 1 minute. Drain.

Return carrots and green beans to pot; heat over medium heat. Add butter, honey, salt and pepper; cook, stirring, until glazed, about 1 minute. Remove from heat. Stir in parsley. Serve with pork.

NUTRITIONAL INFORMATION PER SERVING about 278 cal, 24 g pro, 13 g total fat (5 g sat. fat), 17 g carb (4 g dietary fibre, 8 g sugar), 69 mg chol, 636 mg sodium, 598 mg potassium. % RDI: 6% calcium, 14% iron, 108% vit A, 23% vit C, 20% folate.

LEMONGRASS PORK TENDERLOIN

400 g	pork tenderloin, trimmed
¼ cup	vegetable oil, divided
¼ tsp	grated lime zest
2 tbsp	lime juice
1 tbsp	grated fresh ginger
1 tbsp	grated lemongrass
2	cloves garlic, minced
½ tsp	liquid honey
½ tsp	salt
¼ tsp	pepper
1 tbsp	chopped fresh cilantro or fresh parsley

HONEYED CARROTS & BEANS

1	bunch carrots (about 300 g total), sliced diagonally
400 g	green beans, trimmed
2 tbsp	butter
1 tbsp	liquid honey
¾ tsp	each salt and pepper
2 tbsp	chopped fresh parsley

MAKE IT A MEAL

Lemongrass Pork Tenderloin With Honeyed Carrots & Beans	278 cal
Add: ½ cup prepared couscous	88 cal
Total	**366 cal**

MAKES 6 SERVINGS
HANDS-ON TIME 25 MINUTES
COOKING TIME 6 HOURS
TOTAL TIME 6½ HOURS

Spiced Pork Stew

1 tbsp	pickling spices
1	bay leaf
1 kg	boneless pork shoulder blade roast
½ tsp	each salt and pepper
2 tbsp	vegetable oil
1	onion, sliced
2	ribs celery, chopped
2	cloves garlic, minced
2 cups	quartered mushrooms
⅓ cup	tomato paste
1 cup	dry red wine
1	796 ml can stewed tomatoes
2 tbsp	finely chopped fresh mint (or 2 tsp dried)
2 tbsp	chopped fresh parsley

Cut 5-inch square of double-thickness cheesecloth. Place pickling spices and bay leaf in centre; tie with string into bundle. Place in slow cooker.

Trim and cut pork into 1-inch cubes; toss with salt and pepper. In Dutch oven or heavy-bottomed pot, heat oil over medium-high heat; working in batches, cook pork, stirring, until browned, about 5 minutes. Add to slow cooker.

Drain any fat from pot. Add onion, celery, garlic and mushrooms; cook over medium heat, stirring occasionally, until softened, about 5 minutes.

Add tomato paste; cook, stirring, for 2 minutes. Stir in wine and tomatoes, scraping up any brown bits and breaking up tomatoes with spoon; bring to boil. Add to slow cooker.

Cover and cook on low for 6 to 8 hours or until tender. Discard spice bundle. Stir in mint; sprinkle with parsley.

NUTRITIONAL INFORMATION PER SERVING about 293 cal, 28 g pro, 13 g total fat (3 g sat. fat), 16 g carb (3 g dietary fibre), 76 mg chol, 662 mg sodium. % RDI: 9% calcium, 26% iron, 12% vit A, 48% vit C, 11% folate.

MAKE IT A MEAL

Spiced Pork Stew	293 cal
Add: ½ cup basmati rice	103 cal
Total	**396 cal**

Mustard-Glazed Pork Skewers
With Grilled Sweet Potatoes

MAKES 4 SERVINGS
HANDS-ON TIME 30 MINUTES
TOTAL TIME 30 MINUTES

In shallow saucepan, pour enough water to come 1 inch up side of pan; bring to gentle simmer. Place sweet potato in steamer insert; set in pan. Cover and steam until tender, about 10 minutes. Transfer sweet potatoes to baking sheet. Brush with 2 tsp of the oil; sprinkle with thyme and half each of the salt and pepper. Set aside.

Meanwhile, stir together grainy mustard, hot mustard, honey and garlic; set aside.

In bowl, toss pork with onion, 1 tbsp of the mustard mixture, the remaining 1 tsp oil and remaining salt and pepper. Alternating pork and onion, thread onto metal or soaked wooden skewers.

Place skewers and sweet potatoes on greased grill over medium-high heat; close lid and grill, turning once and brushing skewers with remaining mustard mixture, until potatoes are tender and juices run clear when pork is pierced, about 10 minutes.

NUTRITIONAL INFORMATION PER SERVING about 328 cal, 28 g pro, 7 g total fat (2 g sat. fat), 39 g carb (5 g dietary fibre, 15 g sugar), 61 mg chol, 394 mg sodium, 833 mg potassium. % RDI: 7% calcium, 20% iron, 277% vit A, 40% vit C, 10% folate.

2	medium sweet potatoes (about 800 g total), peeled and cut crosswise in ½-inch slices
1 tbsp	olive oil, divided
1 tsp	chopped fresh thyme
¼ tsp	each salt and pepper
2 tbsp	grainy mustard
1 tbsp	hot mustard
2 tsp	liquid honey
1	clove garlic, minced
450 g	pork tenderloin, trimmed and cut in ¾-inch cubes
half	red onion, cut in 1-inch chunks

TEST KITCHEN TIP

Instead of steaming the sweet potatoes, you can pierce them with a fork and microwave on high, turning once, until tender-crisp, about 4 minutes. Let them cool slightly, and then peel, slice and grill as directed.

MAKES 4 SERVINGS
HANDS-ON TIME 25 MINUTES
TOTAL TIME 25 MINUTES

Tomato & Pancetta Pasta

225 g	rigatoni (about 3 cups)
120 g	pancetta, diced (about 1 cup)
4	cloves garlic, sliced
half	bulb fennel, trimmed, finely chopped and fronds reserved
¼ tsp	each salt and pepper
1	225 g pkg vine-ripened cherry tomatoes
1	225 g pkg mixed cherry tomatoes, halved
2 tbsp	extra-virgin olive oil
1 tbsp	red wine vinegar

In large pot of boiling water, cook pasta according to package directions. Reserving 1 cup of the cooking liquid, drain.

Meanwhile, in large skillet, cook pancetta over medium heat, stirring occasionally, until crisp, about 6 minutes. Scrape into bowl.

Drain all but 3 tbsp fat from pan; cook garlic, chopped fennel, salt and pepper over medium heat, stirring often, until fennel is softened, about 4 minutes. Stir in tomatoes and oil; cook, stirring, until tomatoes are slightly softened, about 3 minutes. Stir in vinegar.

Stir in pasta and ½ cup of the reserved cooking liquid; simmer, adding more cooking liquid if needed to coat pasta, until sauce is thickened, 1 to 2 minutes. Remove from heat; divide among plates. Sprinkle with pancetta; garnish with fennel fronds.

NUTRITIONAL INFORMATION PER SERVING about 388 cal, 12 g pro, 15 g total fat (3 g sat. fat), 51 g carb (5 g dietary fibre, 6 g sugar), 16 mg chol, 528 mg sodium, 510 mg potassium. % RDI: 3% calcium, 18% iron, 12% vit A, 38% vit C, 55% folate.

Slow Cooker Smoked Sausage Minestrone

MAKES 12 SERVINGS
HANDS-ON TIME 15 MINUTES
COOKING TIME 6¼ HOURS
TOTAL TIME 6½ HOURS

In slow cooker, combine sausage, broth, water, carrots, celery, onion, parsley sprigs, bay leaves, Italian seasoning and pepper; cover and cook on low until vegetables are tender, 6 to 8 hours.

Discard parsley and bay leaves; using slotted spoon, transfer sausage to cutting board. Add red pepper, peas and pasta to slow cooker; cover and cook on high until red pepper is tender and pasta is al dente, 15 to 20 minutes.

Meanwhile, slice sausage crosswise into rounds; return to slow cooker. Ladle soup into bowls; sprinkle with chopped parsley (if using).

NUTRITIONAL INFORMATION PER SERVING about 336 cal, 25 g pro, 10 g total fat (4 g sat. fat), 37 g carb (4 g dietary fibre, 8 g sugar), 51 mg chol, 744 mg sodium, 593 mg potassium. % RDI: 6% calcium, 14% iron, 70% vit A, 125% vit C, 18% folate.

450 g	smoked sausage (such as kielbasa)
4 cups	sodium-reduced chicken broth
2 cups	water,
1½ cups	chopped carrots
1½ cups	chopped celery
1	onion, diced
8	sprigs fresh parsley
2	bay leaves
2 tsp	Italian herb seasoning
½ tsp	pepper
1	sweet red pepper, diced
1 cup	frozen peas
1 cup	tubetti or orzo
¼ cup	chopped fresh parsley (optional)

TEST KITCHEN TIP

If you're reheating leftover minestrone, you may need to thin it with a little extra broth.

MAKES 8 SERVINGS
HANDS-ON TIME 15 MINUTES
TOTAL TIME 30 MINUTES

White Bean & Kale Soup

300 g	salami, casings removed, halved lengthwise and thinly sliced crosswise
2	leeks (white and light green parts only), chopped
2	carrots, thinly sliced
3	cloves garlic, minced
1 tbsp	each dried oregano and dried sage
4 cups	sodium-reduced chicken broth
2½ cups	water
2	540 ml cans sodium-reduced cannellini beans, drained and rinsed
6 cups	thinly sliced stemmed kale
2 tbsp	lemon juice (approx)
	shaved Parmesan cheese (optional)
1 tsp	extra-virgin olive oil (optional)

In Dutch oven or large heavy-bottomed pot, cook salami over medium heat until browned, 4 to 6 minutes; using slotted spoon, transfer to bowl. Set aside.

In same pot, cook leeks and carrots until softened, 3 to 5 minutes; stir in garlic, oregano and sage. Add broth and water; bring to boil. Reduce heat, cover and simmer for 10 minutes.

Increase heat to medium; stir in salami, beans and kale. Simmer for 5 minutes. Remove from heat; add lemon juice, adding up to 1 tbsp more lemon juice to taste. Add Parmesan (if using) and drizzle with oil (if using).

NUTRITIONAL INFORMATION PER SERVING about 304 cal, 18 g pro, 15 g total fat (5 g sat. fat), 27 g carb (9 g dietary fibre, 5 g sugar), 30 mg chol, 1,014 mg sodium, 582 mg potassium. % RDI: 10% calcium, 21% iron, 68% vit A, 30% vit C, 33% folate.

TEST KITCHEN TIP

For a vegetarian version of this soup, omit the salami, cooking the leeks and carrots in 1 tbsp olive oil and using vegetable broth instead of chicken broth. If you're doing this, be sure to adjust the seasoning to taste.

Potato, Chorizo & Rapini Soup

MAKES 6 TO 8 SERVINGS
HANDS-ON TIME 30 MINUTES
TOTAL TIME 35 MINUTES

Trim ½ inch from ends of rapini stems; cut rapini crosswise into thirds, separating leaves and stems. Set aside.

In Dutch oven or large heavy-bottomed pot, heat oil over medium heat; cook onion and sausage, stirring often, until onion is beginning to soften, about 2 minutes. Add potatoes; cook, stirring occasionally and adding up to ⅓ cup water as needed if potatoes begin to stick to bottom of pot, about 8 minutes.

Add garlic, paprika and hot pepper flakes; cook, stirring, until fragrant, about 1 minute. Stir in broth and 3 cups water; bring to boil. Reduce heat and simmer, stirring occasionally, until potatoes are tender, about 15 minutes.

Meanwhile, in large saucepan of boiling water, cook rapini stems for 2 minutes. Stir in leaves; cook until stems are tender-crisp and leaves are wilted, about 1 minute. Drain. Stir rapini, lemon juice, salt and pepper into soup.

NUTRITIONAL INFORMATION PER EACH OF 8 SERVINGS about 174 cal, 8 g pro, 8 g total fat (3 g sat. fat), 18 g carb (2 g dietary fibre, 2 g sugar), 15 mg chol, 587 mg sodium, 395 mg potassium. % RDI: 5% calcium, 9% iron, 8% vit A, 18% vit C, 12% folate.

250 g	rapini (about half bunch)
1 tbsp	olive oil
1	onion, chopped
¾ cup	chopped dry-cured chorizo sausage
700 g	yellow-fleshed potatoes (about 5), peeled and cut in ½-inch cubes
3⅓ cups	water (approx)
4	cloves garlic, minced
1 tsp	sweet paprika
¼ tsp	hot pepper flakes
3 cups	sodium-reduced chicken broth
4 tsp	lemon juice
½ tsp	salt
pinch	pepper

TEST KITCHEN TIP

Prepping potatoes ahead of time? Submerge them in water after peeling their skins—the water slows down the natural (and harmless) oxidizing that can turn potatoes pink or brown.

Tomato & Bean Soup
With Crispy Bacon

MAKES 6 SERVINGS
HANDS-ON TIME 35 MINUTES
TOTAL TIME 35 MINUTES

3	strips bacon, thinly sliced
1	small onion, diced
1 cup	diced celery
1 cup	diced carrot
3	cloves garlic, minced
½ tsp	each granulated sugar, dried oregano and ground fennel seeds
¼ tsp	each salt and pepper
pinch	cayenne pepper
2 tbsp	tomato paste
2 cups	sodium-reduced chicken broth
1½ cups	bottled strained tomatoes (passata)
1 cup	water
1	540 ml can cannellini beans, drained and rinsed
¼ cup	crumbled feta cheese
2 tbsp	chopped fresh chives

In Dutch oven or large heavy-bottomed pot, cook bacon over medium heat, stirring often, until bacon is crisp, about 4 minutes. Using slotted spoon, transfer to paper towel–lined plate. Set aside.

Drain all but 1 tbsp fat from pot; cook onion and celery over medium heat, stirring occasionally, until onion is softened, about 3 minutes. Add carrot; cook, stirring often, for 4 minutes. Add garlic, sugar, oregano, fennel seeds, salt, pepper and cayenne pepper; cook, stirring, until fragrant, about 1 minute.

Stir in tomato paste until combined. Stir in broth, strained tomatoes and water; bring to boil. Stir in beans; reduce heat and simmer, stirring occasionally, until slightly thickened and celery is softened, 15 to 20 minutes. Ladle into serving bowls; sprinkle with bacon, feta and chives.

NUTRITIONAL INFORMATION PER SERVING about 175 cal, 9 g pro, 6 g total fat (2 g sat. fat), 22 g carb (6 g dietary fibre, 8 g sugar), 12 mg chol, 733 mg sodium, 484 mg potassium. % RDI: 9% calcium, 19% iron, 35% vit A, 10% vit C, 14% folate.

TEST KITCHEN TIP

Passata is a purée of lightly cooked tomatoes that's strained to remove skins and seeds. You'll find it in jars, near the canned tomatoes in your grocery store.

Potato, Chorizo &
Rapini Soup
Page 83

Tomato & Bean Soup
With Crispy Bacon

Tomato & Fennel Poached Tilapia

MAKES 4 SERVINGS
HANDS-ON TIME 30 MINUTES
TOTAL TIME 30 MINUTES

Trim fennel, reserving fronds. Quarter fennel lengthwise; remove core. Thinly slice fennel lengthwise.

In large skillet, heat oil over medium heat; cook sliced fennel, onion, fennel seeds and hot pepper flakes, stirring, until fennel is softened, about 10 minutes.

Stir in strained tomatoes and water; bring to boil. Reduce heat and simmer for 5 minutes.

Sprinkle fish with salt and pepper; add to fennel mixture. Cover and cook over medium-low heat until fish flakes easily when tested, about 8 minutes.

Meanwhile, add couscous to heatproof bowl; pour in boiling water. Cover and let stand until no liquid remains, about 10 minutes. Fluff with fork. Serve topped with fish and sauce. Garnish with tarragon and reserved fennel fronds.

NUTRITIONAL INFORMATION PER SERVING about 388 cal, 31 g pro, 7 g total fat (1 g sat. fat), 52 g carb (8 g dietary fibre, 9 g sugar), 57 mg chol, 721 mg sodium, 1,044 mg potassium. % RDI: 8% calcium, 42% iron, 1% vit A, 17% vit C, 25% folate.

1	bulb fennel
1 tbsp	olive oil
1	onion, thinly sliced
1 tsp	fennel seeds, crushed
pinch	hot pepper flakes
1	680 ml bottle strained tomatoes (passata)
¼ cup	water
450 g	tilapia fillets (about 2), quartered
½ tsp	salt
¼ tsp	pepper
1 cup	whole wheat couscous
1¼ cups	boiling water
1 tbsp	chopped fresh tarragon

TEST KITCHEN TIP

Whole wheat couscous adds a fibre boost to this dish, and it cooks almost as quickly as regular couscous.

Buttery Halibut
With Balsamic Cherry Tomatoes & Arugula Salad

MAKES 4 SERVINGS
HANDS-ON TIME 15 MINUTES
TOTAL TIME 15 MINUTES

HALIBUT WITH BALSAMIC TOMATOES

2 tbsp	olive oil, divided
1½ cups	cubed sourdough bread
1	255 g pkg cherry tomatoes
1	clove garlic, finely grated or pressed
2 tsp	balsamic vinegar
¼ tsp	each salt and pepper, divided
4	skinless halibut fillets (about 450 g total)
1 tbsp	butter

ARUGULA SALAD

2 tbsp	olive oil
1 tbsp	lemon juice
½ tsp	liquid honey
pinch	each salt and pepper
6 cups	lightly packed baby arugula
¼ cup	thinly sliced red onion
⅓ cup	shaved Parmesan cheese

HALIBUT WITH BALSAMIC TOMATOES In large nonstick skillet, heat 1 tbsp of the oil over medium heat; cook bread, stirring occasionally, until crisp and light golden, about 3 minutes. Scrape into bowl. Set aside.

In same pan, heat 2 tsp of the remaining oil over medium heat; cook tomatoes and garlic, stirring, until tomatoes are beginning to shrivel, about 2 minutes. Stir in vinegar and half each of the salt and pepper; cook, stirring, until fragrant, about 1 minute. Scrape into bowl with bread; toss to combine. Set aside.

Sprinkle fish with remaining salt and pepper. In same pan, heat remaining 1 tsp oil over medium-high heat; cook fish, turning once, until golden and flakes easily when tested, about 7 minutes. Add butter; cook, swirling pan, until butter is melted and fish is coated. Transfer to plate.

ARUGULA SALAD While fish is cooking, in large bowl, whisk together oil, lemon juice, honey, salt and pepper. Add arugula, red onion and Parmesan; toss to coat. Divide among serving plates; top with bread mixture and fish.

NUTRITIONAL INFORMATION PER SERVING about 375 cal, 29 g pro, 21 g total fat (5 g sat. fat), 16 g carb (2 g dietary fibre, 5 g sugar), 48 mg chol, 453 mg sodium, 870 mg potassium. % RDI: 18% calcium, 17% iron, 22% vit A, 27% vit C, 34% folate.

TEST KITCHEN TIP

If you prefer, use any firm, white-fleshed fish instead of halibut. Cod, pickerel and tilapia are good options.

Herbed Salmon & Potato Frittata

MAKES 8 SERVINGS
HANDS-ON TIME 15 MINUTES
TOTAL TIME 30 MINUTES

Stir together basil, chives and dill; set aside.

In 10-inch ovenproof or cast-iron skillet, heat oil over medium heat, brushing up side of pan. Cook potato with a pinch each of the salt and pepper, stirring, until light golden, about 5 minutes. Add garlic; cook, stirring, until fragrant, about 1 minute.

Meanwhile, in bowl, beat eggs; stir in remaining salt and pepper and all but 1 tbsp of the basil mixture. Pour over potato mixture; reduce heat to medium-low and cook until bottom and side are set but top is still slightly runny, about 15 minutes.

Broil until top is golden and set, about 2 minutes. Top with smoked salmon and sour cream. Sprinkle with remaining basil mixture.

NUTRITIONAL INFORMATION PER SERVING about 161 cal, 12 g pro, 9 g total fat (3 g sat. fat), 6 g carb (1 g dietary fibre, 1 g sugar), 235 mg chol, 393 mg sodium, 215 mg potassium. % RDI: 4% calcium, 9% iron, 14% vit A, 5% vit C, 18% folate.

¼ cup	chopped fresh basil
3 tbsp	each chopped fresh chives and fresh dill
1 tbsp	olive oil
1½ cups	diced peeled cooked red or white waxy potato (about 1 large)
½ tsp	each salt and pepper, divided
2	cloves garlic, minced
10	large eggs
170 g	smoked salmon
2 tbsp	sour cream

TEST KITCHEN TIP

If your skillet handle is not ovenproof, wrap it in foil before placing the skillet under the broiler.

Blackened Arctic Char
With Asparagus Orzo

MAKES 4 SERVINGS
HANDS-ON TIME 20 MINUTES
TOTAL TIME 20 MINUTES

BLACKENED ARCTIC CHAR

2 tbsp	sweet paprika
2 tsp	each dried thyme and dried oregano
1½ tsp	chili powder
pinch	cayenne pepper
4	skin-on arctic char fillets (about 450 g total)
¼ tsp	each salt and pepper
1 tbsp	olive oil

ASPARAGUS ORZO

1 cup	orzo
1	bunch asparagus (about 450 g), trimmed and cut in 1½-inch lengths
2 tbsp	grated Parmesan cheese
¼ tsp	grated lemon zest
1 tbsp	lemon juice
2 tsp	unsalted butter
¼ tsp	each salt and pepper
2 tbsp	torn fresh basil, divided

BLACKENED ARCTIC CHAR In shallow dish, stir together paprika, thyme, oregano, chili powder and cayenne pepper. Sprinkle fish with salt and pepper; dredge in paprika mixture, turning to coat both sides and shaking off excess.

In large nonstick skillet, heat oil over medium-high heat; cook fish, turning once, until dark golden, about 4 minutes. Reduce heat to medium; cook, turning once, until fish flakes easily when tested, 3 to 5 minutes.

ASPARAGUS ORZO While fish is cooking, in large pot of boiling lightly salted water, cook pasta for 2 minutes less than package directions for al dente. Add asparagus; cook until pasta is al dente and asparagus is tender-crisp, about 2 minutes. Reserving ¼ cup of the cooking liquid, drain. Return pasta mixture to pot.

Stir in Parmesan, lemon zest, lemon juice, butter, salt, pepper and enough of the reserved cooking liquid to lightly coat pasta. Stir in 1 tbsp of the basil. Divide among serving plates; top with Blackened Arctic Char. Sprinkle with remaining 1 tbsp basil.

NUTRITIONAL INFORMATION PER SERVING about 379 cal, 32 g pro, 11 g total fat (3 g sat. fat), 40 g carb (5 g dietary fibre, 2 g sugar), 74 mg chol, 809 mg sodium, 750 mg potassium. % RDI: 10% calcium, 29% iron, 34% vit A, 25% vit C, 79% folate.

TEST KITCHEN TIP

You can replace arctic char with salmon (a close relative), but choose fish raised in recirculating aquaculture systems if you're concerned about sustainability.

Peruvian-Style Halibut Ceviche

MAKES 4 TO 6 SERVINGS
HANDS-ON TIME 5 MINUTES
REFRIGERATION TIME 30 MINUTES
TOTAL TIME 35 MINUTES

In ceramic or glass bowl, mix together fish, Thai pepper, corn, red onion, lime juice, orange zest, orange juice, ginger and salt; cover with plastic wrap. Refrigerate, stirring occasionally, until fish is opaque throughout, about 30 minutes. Sprinkle with cilantro before serving.

NUTRITIONAL INFORMATION PER EACH OF 6 SERVINGS about 110 cal, 15 g pro, 1 g total fat (trace sat. fat), 10 g carb (1 g dietary fibre, 2 g sugar), 37 mg chol, 187 mg sodium, 458 mg potassium. % RDI: 1% calcium, 3% iron, 5% vit A, 20% vit C, 13% folate.

450 g	skinless halibut fillet, cut in ¾-inch cubes and patted dry
1	Thai bird's-eye pepper, thinly sliced
1 cup	cooked corn kernels, cooled
½ cup	thinly sliced red onion
¼ cup	lime juice
2 tsp	orange zest
¼ cup	orange juice
1 tsp	minced fresh ginger
½ tsp	kosher salt
½ cup	chopped fresh cilantro

TEST KITCHEN TIP

Always choose the freshest fish possible for ceviche and mix ingredients in a ceramic or glass "non-reactive" bowl. The acid in the lime juice will react with a metal bowl, imparting a metallic taste to the fish.

Soy-Maple Glazed Salmon & Swiss Chard

MAKES 4 SERVINGS
HANDS-ON TIME 15 MINUTES
TOTAL TIME 20 MINUTES

1	large bunch rainbow Swiss chard (about 340 g)
5	cloves garlic
3 tbsp	maple syrup
2 tbsp	sodium-reduced soy sauce
4	skinless salmon fillets (about 450 g total)
	salt and pepper
4 tsp	olive oil, divided

Cut stems from Swiss chard; coarsely chop leaves. Trim and cut stems into ½-inch thick pieces. Set aside separately.

Finely grate or press 2 garlic cloves; mince remaining garlic. Set minced garlic aside.

In small bowl, stir together grated garlic, the maple syrup and soy sauce. Set aside.

Sprinkle fish with pinch each salt and pepper. In nonstick skillet, heat 2 tsp of the oil over medium heat; cook fish for 4 minutes. Turn fish and brush with 2 tbsp of the maple syrup mixture; cook until fish flakes easily when tested. Transfer to serving dish; tent with foil. Wipe pan clean.

In same pan, heat remaining 2 tsp oil over medium heat; cook minced garlic, stirring, until fragrant, about 30 seconds. Add Swiss chard stems and pinch each salt and pepper; cook, stirring, until tender-crisp, about 4 minutes. Add Swiss chard leaves; cook, stirring occasionally, until leaves are softened and beginning to wilt, about 2 minutes. Stir in 1 tbsp of the maple syrup mixture. Scrape into separate serving dish.

Add remaining maple syrup mixture to pan; cook over medium heat until thickened, about 2 minutes. Spoon over fish. Serve with Swiss chard.

NUTRITIONAL INFORMATION PER SERVING about 282 cal, 21 g pro, 16 g total fat (3 g sat. fat), 14 g carb (1 g dietary fibre, 9 g sugar), 55 mg chol, 497 mg sodium, 649 mg potassium. % RDI: 6% calcium, 14% iron, 40% vit A, 30% vit C, 17% folate.

TEST KITCHEN TIP

Swiss chard is a leafy green member of the beet family, with a flavour similar to spinach when cooked. Raw Swiss chard is a good alternative to kale or lettuce, especially in make-ahead salads; its sturdy leaves are more tender than kale, but resist wilting when dressed with vinaigrette.

Sheet Pan Mediterranean Salmon

Cover

MAKES 4 SERVINGS
HANDS-ON TIME 15 MINUTES
TOTAL TIME 25 MINUTES

Preheat oven to 425°F. Line baking sheet with parchment paper.

SHALLOT VINAIGRETTE In bowl, whisk together oil, vinegar, mustard, shallot, salt and pepper. Reserve ¼ cup in small bowl.

Arrange salmon, skin side down, on prepared pan; sprinkle with salt and pepper. Scatter haricots verts and cherry tomatoes around fish; drizzle vegetables with remaining Shallot Vinaigrette, tossing to coat.

Bake until fish flakes easily when tested and vegetables are tender, 12 to 15 minutes. Flake fish into large pieces. Sprinkle with parsley, olives and caper berries (if using). Divide fish and vegetables among plates; drizzle with reserved ¼ cup Shallot Vinaigrette, if desired.

NUTRITIONAL INFORMATION PER SERVING about 312 cal, 22 g pro, 21 g total fat (4 g sat. fat), 10 g carb (3 g dietary fibre, 4 g sugar), 54 mg chol, 402 mg sodium, 713 mg potassium. % RDI: 6% calcium, 10% iron, 18% vit A, 47% vit C, 31% folate.

SHALLOT VINAIGRETTE

¼ **cup**	olive oil
3 tbsp	white wine vinegar
1 tbsp	grainy mustard
1	shallot, finely chopped
½ tsp	each salt and pepper
1	skin-on salmon fillet (about 500 g)
¼ tsp	each salt and pepper
3 cups	haricots verts, trimmed
3 cups	cherry tomatoes
¼ cup	chopped parsley
¼ cup	pitted black olives (such as Kalamata or Niçoise), halved
	caper berries (optional)

MAKES 4 SERVINGS
HANDS-ON TIME 15 MINUTES
TOTAL TIME 15 MINUTES

Salmon Maki Quinoa Bowls

2 cups	water
1 cup	quinoa, rinsed
2 tsp	sesame oil, divided
3	green onions, thinly sliced (light and dark green parts separated)
4 tsp	grated fresh ginger
2	cloves garlic, finely grated or pressed
¼ tsp	salt
150 g	smoked salmon
1	avocado, peeled, pitted and sliced
half	sweet red pepper, julienned
quarter	cucumber, halved lengthwise and thinly sliced crosswise
1 tsp	sesame seeds
4 tsp	sodium-reduced soy sauce
½ tsp	prepared wasabi

In saucepan, bring water to boil; stir in quinoa. Return to boil; reduce heat to low, cover and cook until tender, about 12 minutes. Remove from heat; fluff with fork.

In nonstick skillet, heat 1 tsp of the sesame oil over medium heat; cook light parts of green onions, the ginger and garlic, stirring, until fragrant, about 1 minute. Stir in quinoa and salt; cook, stirring, for 2 minutes.

Divide quinoa mixture among serving bowls. Top with fish, avocado, red pepper, cucumber, dark parts of green onions and the sesame seeds.

Whisk together soy sauce, wasabi and remaining 1 tsp sesame oil; drizzle over bowls.

NUTRITIONAL INFORMATION PER SERVING about 299 cal, 14 g pro, 12 g total fat (2 g sat. fat), 34 g carb (7 g dietary fibre, 3 g sugar), 9 mg chol, 631 mg sodium, 583 mg potassium. % RDI: 4% calcium, 21% iron, 7% vit A, 40% vit C, 45% folate.

TEST KITCHEN TIP

For added flavour, sprinkle with furikake, a Japanese topping for rice dishes. Furikake typically includes dried fish, seaweed, sesame seeds, salt, sugar and MSG.

Warm Potato Salad
With Smoked Trout

MAKES 4 TO 6 SERVINGS
HANDS-ON TIME 20 MINUTES
TOTAL TIME 25 MINUTES

In large pot of boiling salted water, cook potatoes until fork-tender, about 10 minutes. Drain. Let cool for 10 minutes. Cut in half.

While potatoes are cooking, using fork, coarsely flake fish. Set aside.

In large bowl, whisk together oil, lemon zest, lemon juice, dill, garlic, horseradish, salt and pepper.

Add potatoes, lettuce, radishes, red onion and capers; gently toss to coat. Top with fish.

NUTRITIONAL INFORMATION PER EACH OF 6 SERVINGS about 243 cal, 13 g pro, 12 g total fat (2 g sat. fat), 20 g carb (3 g dietary fibre, 2 g sugar), 24 mg chol, 800 mg sodium, 550 mg potassium. % RDI: 3% calcium, 9% iron, 15% vit A, 39% vit C, 15% folate.

680 g	mini red-skinned potatoes
300 g	hot-smoked trout, skin removed
¼ cup	extra-virgin olive oil
¼ tsp	grated lemon zest
2 tbsp	lemon juice
1 tbsp	chopped fresh dill
1	clove garlic, finely grated or pressed
1 tsp	prepared horseradish
¼ tsp	each salt and pepper
4 cups	chopped green leaf lettuce
4	radishes, trimmed and thinly sliced
half	small red onion, thinly sliced
1 tbsp	capers, drained, rinsed and finely chopped

TEST KITCHEN TIP

Hot-smoked trout is less expensive than cold-smoked trout. Look for hot-smoked trout in your supermarket in the refrigerated seafood section or alongside cured meats. If the package doesn't specify, check the colour of the fish: Cold-smoked trout is a bright, shiny reddish-orange, while hot-smoked is matte and a duller shade of pink or tan.

MAKES 4 SERVINGS
HANDS-ON TIME 20 MINUTES
TOTAL TIME 30 MINUTES

Tuna & Potato Salad
With Lemon-Caper Dressing

LEMON-CAPER DRESSING

3 tbsp	lemon juice
4 tsp	chopped drained capers
1 tbsp	grainy mustard
2 tsp	liquid honey
½ tsp	each salt and pepper
⅓ cup	olive oil

SALAD

690 g	mini red-skinned potatoes
8 cups	sliced or torn Little Gem or romaine lettuce
150 g	oil-packed solid light albacore tuna, drained and broken in chunks
1 cup	shredded radicchio
2	shallots, thinly sliced

LEMON-CAPER DRESSING In small bowl, whisk together lemon juice, capers, mustard, honey, salt and pepper. Slowly whisk in oil. Set aside.

SALAD In large pot of boiling salted water, cook potatoes until fork-tender, about 10 minutes. Drain and let cool for 10 minutes. Cut in half.

In large bowl, gently toss together potatoes, lettuce, tuna, radicchio, shallots and dressing.

NUTRITIONAL INFORMATION PER SERVING about 379 cal, 12 g pro, 21 g total fat (3 g sat. fat), 39 g carb (6 g dietary fibre, 7 g sugar), 7 mg chol, 991 mg sodium, 1,157 mg potassium. % RDI: 6% calcium, 21% iron, 85% vit A, 90% vit C, 78% folate.

TEST KITCHEN TIP

For this recipe, we prefer good-quality oil-packed tuna, which has more moisture and flavour. Water-packed tuna, which has fewer calories, will work too.

Stir-Fried Seafood Udon Noodles

MAKES 4 SERVINGS
HANDS-ON TIME 20 MINUTES
TOTAL TIME 20 MINUTES

In large nonstick skillet or wok, heat 2 tsp of the oil over medium-high heat; cook shrimp and scallops, stirring frequently, just until shrimp are pink and scallops are opaque, about 3 minutes. Transfer to plate; set aside.

In same pan, heat remaining 2 tsp oil over medium-high heat; cook ginger and garlic, stirring, until fragrant, about 1 minute. Add noodles, bok choy, mushrooms, red pepper, green onions and water; cook, stirring, until noodles are softened, about 4 minutes. Add shrimp, scallops, oyster sauce and pepper; cook, stirring, until combined.

NUTRITIONAL INFORMATION PER SERVING about 316 cal, 25 g pro, 7 g total fat (1 g sat. fat), 41 g carb (4 g dietary fibre, 3 g sugar), 78 mg chol, 638 mg sodium, 833 mg potassium. % RDI: 14% calcium, 23% iron, 59% vit A, 162% vit C, 29% folate.

4 tsp	vegetable oil, divided
225 g	jumbo shrimp (21 to 25 count), peeled and deveined
225 g	jumbo scallops (20 to 40 count), patted dry
1 tbsp	minced peeled fresh ginger
2	cloves garlic, minced
2	200 g pkgs fresh udon noodles
4	heads Shanghai bok choy (about 450 g total), cut in ½-inch wedges
2 cups	sliced stemmed shiitake mushrooms
1	sweet red pepper, thinly sliced
2	green onions, sliced diagonally in ½-inch thick pieces
⅔ cup	water
2 tbsp	oyster sauce
¼ tsp	pepper

TEST KITCHEN TIP

Udon noodles are a real timesaver for easy weeknight dinners. There's no need to boil them; just separate the noodles by hand, then add them directly to stir-fries or soups.

MAKES 4 TO 6 SERVINGS
HANDS-ON TIME 25 MINUTES
TOTAL TIME 25 MINUTES

Mixed Seafood Cataplana

450 g	littleneck clams
450 g	mussels
150 g	shell-on jumbo shrimp (21 to 25 count/about 8 total)
2 tbsp	extra-virgin olive oil (approx)
150 g	dry-cured chorizo sausage, chopped
2	shallots, thinly sliced
2	cloves garlic, minced
¼ tsp	smoked paprika (approx)
¼ tsp	salt
pinch	pepper
2	plum tomatoes, chopped
½ cup	dry white wine
½ cup	clam juice
¼ cup	fresh parsley leaves

Using stiff brush, scrub clams and mussels; remove any beards. Discard any that have cracked shells or do not close when tapped. Peel and devein shrimp, leaving tails intact.

In Dutch oven or large heavy-bottomed pot, heat oil over medium heat; cook sausage, stirring, until beginning to brown, about 2 minutes. Add shallots, garlic, paprika, salt and pepper; cook, stirring, until fragrant and shallots are beginning to soften, about 1 minute. Stir in tomatoes, wine and clam juice; bring to boil. Cook, stirring occasionally, until slightly reduced, 3 to 4 minutes.

Add clams; cover and cook for 2 minutes. Add mussels and shrimp, gently shaking pot to distribute evenly; cover and cook until mussels and clams have opened and shrimp are pink and opaque throughout, 4 to 5 minutes. Remove from heat.

Discard any mussels or clams that do not open. Sprinkle with parsley; drizzle with more oil and sprinkle with more paprika, if desired.

NUTRITIONAL INFORMATION PER EACH OF 6 SERVINGS about 285 cal, 22 g pro, 17 g total fat (5 g sat. fat), 9 g carb (1 g dietary fibre, 2 g sugar), 83 mg chol, 668 mg sodium, 541 mg potassium. % RDI: 5% calcium, 49% iron, 14% vit A, 25% vit C, 18% folate.

MAKE IT A MEAL

Mixed Seafood Cataplana	285 cal
Add 1 dinner roll	85 cal
Total	**370 cal**

Kung Pao Shrimp

MAKES 4 SERVINGS
HANDS-ON TIME 10 MINUTES
TOTAL TIME 10 MINUTES

In small bowl, whisk together hoisin sauce, vinegar, soy sauce and sesame oil. Set aside.

In large nonstick skillet, heat vegetable oil over medium heat. Add garlic, ginger and hot pepper flakes; cook, stirring, until fragrant, about 3 minutes. Add snap peas; cook for 1 minute. Add shrimp; cook until pink and opaque throughout, 3 to 4 minutes. Add hoisin mixture; toss to coat. Sprinkle with green onions.

NUTRITIONAL INFORMATION PER SERVING about 266 cal, 24 g pro, 13 g total fat (1 g sat. fat), 15 g carb (3 g dietary fibre, 6 g sugar), 152 mg chol, 588 mg sodium, 511 mg potassium. % RDI: 11% calcium, 33% iron, 17% vit A, 72% vit C, 26% folate.

2 tbsp	hoisin sauce
2 tbsp	rice vinegar
4 tsp	soy sauce
1 tbsp	sesame oil
2 tbsp	vegetable oil
3	cloves garlic, minced
1 tbsp	minced peeled fresh ginger
½ tsp	hot pepper flakes
2 cups	sugar snap peas, trimmed
450 g	large shrimp (21 to 25 count), peeled and deveined
6	green onions (white and light green parts only), cut crosswise in 1-inch pieces

VARIATION

Kung Pao Chicken

Prepare recipe as directed, substituting 375 g skinless boneless chicken breasts, cut in thin strips, for the shrimp.

MAKE IT A MEAL

Kung Pao Shrimp	266 cal
Add: ½ cup cooked rice noodles	96 cal
Total	**362 cal**

MAKES 4 SERVINGS
HANDS-ON TIME 20 MINUTES
TOTAL TIME 20 MINUTES

Shrimp Lo Mein

1 cup	sodium-reduced chicken broth
2 tbsp	oyster sauce
1 tbsp	cornstarch
1 tsp	sesame oil
1 tbsp	vegetable oil, divided
450 g	jumbo shrimp (21 to 25 count), peeled and deveined
280 g	fresh steamed chow mein noodles
1	carrot, sliced diagonally
1 cup	snow peas, trimmed and halved diagonally
1 cup	quartered button or cremini mushrooms
3	cloves garlic, minced
3	heads Shanghai bok choy, (about 225 g total), quartered

Stir together broth, oyster sauce, cornstarch and sesame oil. Set aside.

In wok or large nonstick skillet, heat 1 tsp of the vegetable oil over medium-high heat; cook shrimp, stirring, until pink and opaque throughout, about 2 minutes. Transfer to plate.

In large pot of boiling water, cook noodles according to package directions; drain.

Meanwhile, add remaining 2 tsp vegetable oil to wok; cook carrot, snow peas, mushrooms and garlic over medium-high heat, stirring, until garlic is fragrant, about 1 minute. Add bok choy; cook, stirring, just until wilted, about 1 minute. Stir in broth mixture, shrimp and noodles. Cook, tossing, until sauce is thickened and noodles are coated, about 1 minute.

NUTRITIONAL INFORMATION PER SERVING about 361 cal, 27 g pro, 7 g total fat (1 g sat. fat), 46 g carb (3 g dietary fibre, 2 g sugar), 132 mg chol, 646 mg sodium, 578 mg potassium. % RDI: 11% calcium, 36% iron, 63% vit A, 42% vit C, 19% folate.

VARIATION
Tofu Lo Mein

Omit shrimp. Reduce vegetable oil to 2 tsp; use to cook vegetables only. Add 450 g fried tofu balls along with broth mixture. (Look for tofu balls near wonton wrappers and tofu in the refrigerated section of the grocery store.)

Thai Crab Cake Salad
With Red Curry Mayo

MAKES 4 TO 6 SERVINGS
HANDS-ON TIME 30 MINUTES
TOTAL TIME 30 MINUTES

CRAB CAKES In bowl, stir together crabmeat, cilantro, bread crumbs, green onions, egg and curry paste until well combined. Shape into twelve ¾-inch thick patties. *(Make-ahead: Cover and refrigerate for up to 24 hours.)*

In large nonstick skillet, heat oil over medium heat. Working in batches, cook crab cakes, turning once, until firm and golden, about 6 minutes. Transfer to plate; keep warm.

RED CURRY MAYO While crab cakes are cooking, in small bowl, mix mayonnaise with curry paste. Set aside. *(Make-ahead: Cover and refrigerate for up to 2 days.)*

LIME VINAIGRETTE In large bowl, whisk together lime juice, garlic, ginger, honey, salt and pepper. Slowly whisk in oil.

SALAD Add spinach, watercress, avocados and red pepper to vinaigrette; toss to combine. To serve, top with crab cakes and curried mayo.

NUTRITIONAL INFORMATION PER EACH OF 6 SERVINGS about 329 cal, 16 g pro, 24 g total fat (3 g sat. fat), 14 g carb (5 g dietary fibre, 4 g sugar), 87 mg chol, 676 mg sodium, 741 mg potassium. % RDI: 11% calcium, 27% iron, 64% vit A, 102% vit C, 73% folate.

CRAB CAKES

1	tub (454 g) crab claw meat, coarsely chopped
¼ cup	chopped fresh cilantro
¼ cup	dried bread crumbs
2	green onions, chopped
1	egg, lightly beaten
1 tbsp	Thai red curry paste
1 tbsp	vegetable oil

RED CURRY MAYO

3 tbsp	light mayonnaise
1 tsp	Thai red curry paste

LIME VINAIGRETTE

2 tbsp	lime juice
1	clove garlic, finely grated or pressed
1 tsp	grated fresh ginger
1 tsp	liquid honey
pinch	each salt and pepper
¼ cup	vegetable oil

SALAD

12 cups	lightly packed baby spinach
2 cups	lightly packed watercress leaves (about 1 bunch)
2	avocados, peeled, pitted and diced
1	sweet red pepper, diced

TEST KITCHEN TIP

Look for tubs of crabmeat at the deli counter of your grocery store.

Slow Cooker
Curry Coconut Shrimp Soup

MAKES 8 TO 10 SERVINGS
HANDS-ON TIME 15 MINUTES
COOKING TIME 8¼ HOURS
TOTAL TIME 8¼ HOURS

3 cups	sodium-reduced vegetable broth
1	400 ml can coconut milk
2 cups	water
2 tbsp	Thai green curry paste
2 tbsp	minced peeled fresh ginger
3	cloves garlic, thinly sliced
1¼ tsp	salt
2	sweet potatoes, peeled and cut in ½-inch cubes
1	onion, sliced
450 g	jumbo shrimp (21 to 25 count), peeled and deveined
1 cup	frozen corn kernels
2 tbsp	lime juice
1 tbsp	fish sauce
3	green onions, sliced (white and green parts separated)

In slow cooker, whisk together broth, coconut milk, water, curry paste, ginger, garlic and salt. Stir in sweet potatoes and onion; cover and cook on low until sweet potatoes are tender, about 8 hours.

Stir in shrimp and corn; cover and cook on high until shrimp are pink and opaque throughout, about 10 minutes. Stir in lime juice, fish sauce and white parts of green onions. Ladle into serving bowls; sprinkle with green parts of green onions.

PER EACH OF 10 SERVINGS about 191 cal, 9 g pro, 9 g total fat (7 g sat. fat), 20 g carb (3 g dietary fibre, 6 g sugar), 51 mg chol, 791 mg sodium, 408 mg potassium. % RDI: 6% calcium, 21% iron, 104% vit A, 28% vit C, 10% folate.

TEST KITCHEN TIP

We prefer using uncooked frozen shrimp in most recipes. You won't save any time by using cooked frozen shrimp, and its texture and flavour isn't as good as uncooked. Buying deveined shrimp does save time, but take a quick look at each one to be sure the dark vein along the back of the shrimp has been removed completely.

Seafood & Fennel Soup

MAKES 4 TO 6 SERVINGS
HANDS-ON TIME 30 MINUTES
TOTAL TIME 30 MINUTES

In Dutch oven or large heavy-bottomed pot, heat oil over medium heat; cook leeks and garlic, stirring occasionally, until softened, about 5 minutes. Add fennel; cook, stirring, just until softened, about 3 minutes. Stir in water, clam juice, salt and pepper; bring to boil. Reduce heat to gentle simmer; cover and cook until fennel is tender, about 4 minutes.

Increase heat to medium. Stir in scallops; cook just until opaque, about 1 minute. Stir in haddock, parsnip and lemon juice; cook, uncovered and without stirring, until haddock is opaque throughout, about 2 minutes. Spoon into bowls; sprinkle with dill and tarragon.

NUTRITIONAL INFORMATION PER EACH OF 6 SERVINGS about 146 cal, 17 g pro, 3 g total fat (1 g sat. fat), 14 g carb (3 g dietary fibre, 4 g sugar), 39 mg chol, 504 mg sodium, 653 mg potassium. % RDI: 8% calcium, 13% iron, 7% vit A, 22% vit C, 21% folate.

1 tbsp	olive oil
2	leeks (white and light green parts only), halved lengthwise and thinly sliced crosswise
3	cloves garlic, minced
1	bulb fennel, trimmed, cored and thinly sliced
4 cups	water
1	240 ml bottle clam juice
¾ tsp	salt
pinch	pepper
12	jumbo sea scallops (about 250 g total)
250 g	wild haddock or cod fillet, cut in 1-inch chunks
1	parsnip or yellow carrot, thinly sliced in rounds
2 tbsp	lemon juice
1 tbsp	each chopped fresh dill and fresh tarragon

TEST KITCHEN TIP

Be sure to slice the parsnip as thinly as you can, so it can cook as quickly as the haddock.

MAKES 8 TO 10 SERVINGS
HANDS-ON TIME 35 MINUTES
TOTAL TIME 50 MINUTES

Corn & Crab Chowder

4	strips sodium-reduced bacon, chopped
1	sweet onion, diced
2	ribs celery, chopped
1	clove garlic, minced
2 tbsp	all-purpose flour
2	red-skinned potatoes, cubed (about 2¼ cups)
2 cups	sodium-reduced chicken broth
2 cups	water
1 cup	bottled clam juice
½ tsp	dried thyme
½ tsp	smoked paprika
½ tsp	pepper
1	bay leaf
2	227 g pkgs pasteurized crab claw meat, drained
2 cups	frozen corn
⅔ cup	10% cream
1 tbsp	lemon juice

In Dutch oven or large heavy-bottomed pot, cook bacon over medium heat, stirring occasionally, until crisp, about 8 minutes. Using slotted spoon, transfer to paper towel–lined plate. Set aside.

Drain all but 2 tbsp fat from pot; cook onion and celery over medium heat, stirring, until softened, about 8 minutes. Add garlic; cook, stirring, until fragrant, about 1 minute. Sprinkle in flour; cook, stirring, until golden, about 3 minutes.

Stir in potatoes, broth, water, clam juice, thyme, paprika, pepper and bay leaf; bring to boil. Reduce heat, partially cover and simmer for 15 minutes.

Stir in bacon, crabmeat, corn and cream; reduce heat to low and cook, stirring occasionally, until heated through, about 7 minutes. Stir in lemon juice; discard bay leaf.

NUTRITIONAL INFORMATION PER EACH OF 10 SERVINGS about 152 cal, 10 g pro, 5 g total fat (2 g sat. fat), 17 g carb (2 g dietary fibre, 3 g sugar), 38 mg chol, 467 mg sodium, 431 mg potassium. % RDI: 5% calcium, 11% iron, 5% vit A, 15% vit C, 12% folate.

MAKE IT A MEAL

Corn & Crab Chowder	152 cal
Add: Arugula & Mushroom Salad (page 139)	59 cal
Total	**211 cal**

Wine & Bacon Steamed Mussels

MAKES 8 SERVINGS
HANDS-ON TIME 20 MINUTES
TOTAL TIME 25 MINUTES

Scrub mussels; remove any beards. Discard any mussels that do not close when tapped. Set aside.

In Dutch oven or large heavy-bottomed pot over medium heat, cook bacon, stirring occasionally, until crisp, about 5 minutes. Using slotted spoon, transfer to paper towel–lined plate. Set aside.

Drain all but 1 tbsp fat from pot; cook onion, stirring occasionally, until softened, about 5 minutes. Add garlic; cook until fragrant, about 1 minute.

Add wine and bay leaves; bring to boil. Reduce heat; simmer until reduced by half, about 5 minutes. Stir in tomato paste and pepper; return to boil.

Add mussels; cover with tight-fitting lid and steam until mussels open, about 5 minutes. Remove from heat; discard bay leaves and any mussels that do not open. Sprinkle with bacon and parsley.

2 kg	mussels
8	strips bacon, diced
1	large onion, diced
4	cloves garlic, minced
2½ cups	dry white wine
2	bay leaves
2 tbsp	tomato paste
¼ tsp	pepper
2 tbsp	chopped fresh parsley

NUTRITIONAL INFORMATION PER SERVING about 151 cal, 12 g pro, 6 g total fat (2 g sat. fat), 7 g carb (1 g dietary fibre, 2 g sugar), 29 mg chol, 297 mg sodium, 277 mg potassium. % RDI: 3% calcium, 22% iron, 5% vit A, 13% vit C, 15% folate.

TEST KITCHEN TIP

In the grocery store, look for mussels nestled in plenty of ice to keep them fresh. Any with open shells should close quickly when tapped. Mussels should look shiny and wet; if they appear dried out, they may have died or been improperly stored.

MAKES 2 TO 4 SERVINGS
HANDS-ON TIME 15 MINUTES
COOKING TIME 8¼ HOURS
TOTAL TIME 8½ HOURS

Slow Cooker Mussels
In Tomato & Fennel Sauce

900 g	fresh mussels
1	796 ml can diced tomatoes
1	bulb fennel, trimmed, cored and thinly sliced
1 cup	dry red wine
¼ cup	tomato paste
4	cloves garlic, minced
1 tsp	granulated sugar
½ tsp	salt
¼ tsp	pepper
pinch	hot pepper flakes
3 tbsp	35% cream
1 tbsp	chopped fresh tarragon

Scrub mussels; remove any beards. Discard any mussels that do not close when tapped. Set aside.

In slow cooker, combine tomatoes, fennel, wine, tomato paste, garlic, sugar, salt, pepper and hot pepper flakes. Cover and cook on low until fennel is tender, about 8 hours.

Add mussels; cover and cook on high until mussels open, about 15 minutes. Discard any mussels that remain closed. Stir in cream. Sprinkle with tarragon.

NUTRITIONAL INFORMATION PER EACH OF 4 SERVINGS about 173 cal, 12 g pro, 6 g total fat (3 g sat. fat), 21 g carb (4 g dietary fibre, 11 g sugar), 33 mg chol, 721 mg sodium, 956 mg potassium. % RDI: 11% calcium, 39% iron, 12% vit A, 70% vit C, 23% folate.

MAKE IT A MEAL

Slow Cooker Mussels in Tomato & Fennel Sauce	173 cal
Add: Crusty roll	167 cal
Total	**440 cal**

TEST KITCHEN TIP

For a dairy-free version of this recipe, replace the 35% cream with 2 tbsp of extra-virgin olive oil.

Creamy Skillet Mushroom Lasagna

MAKES 6 SERVINGS
HANDS-ON TIME 30 MINUTES
TOTAL TIME 35 MINUTES

6	lasagna noodles (about 2 inches wide), divided
1 tbsp	olive oil
2	227 g pkgs cremini mushrooms, sliced
1	142 g pkg baby spinach (about 5 cups)
¼ tsp	each salt and pepper
2 cups	milk, divided
3 tbsp	all-purpose flour
1 cup	shredded mozzarella cheese, divided
⅔ cup	extra-smooth ricotta cheese
4 tsp	Dijon mustard
pinch	cayenne pepper

In large pot of boiling salted water, cook noodles for 2 minutes less than package directions for al dente; drain. Arrange noodles, keeping edges from touching, in single layer on tea towel.

While noodles are cooking, in nonstick skillet, heat oil over medium-high heat; cook mushrooms, stirring occasionally, until softened and almost no liquid remains, about 7 minutes. Add spinach; cook, stirring, until spinach is beginning to wilt, about 2 minutes. Drain in colander; scrape into bowl. Stir in salt and pepper.

Preheat oven to 425°F. In small saucepan, whisk ¼ cup of the milk with the flour until smooth. Gradually whisk in remaining 1¾ cups milk; cook over medium heat, whisking constantly, until thickened, about 8 minutes. Add ¾ cup of the mozzarella, the ricotta, mustard and cayenne pepper; cook, stirring, until mozzarella is melted. Remove from the heat.

Spoon ½ cup of the sauce into bottom of lightly greased 10-inch cast-iron or ovenproof skillet. Arrange 3 of the noodles over top, trimming ends to fit; top with half of the mushroom mixture. Spoon half of the remaining sauce over top. Arrange remaining 3 noodles, perpendicular to bottom noodles, over top; layer with remaining mushroom mixture and sauce. Sprinkle with remaining ¼ cup mozzarella.

Bake until mozzarella is melted, about 4 minutes; broil until top is golden, about 2 minutes.

NUTRITIONAL INFORMATION PER SERVING about 298 cal, 16 g pro, 13 g total fat (6 g sat. fat), 31 g carb (3 g dietary fibre, 7 g sugar), 31 mg chol, 389 mg sodium, 630 mg potassium. % RDI: 27% calcium, 16% iron, 39% vit A, 3% vit C, 49% folate.

TEST KITCHEN TIP

Cut the cooked noodles with kitchen shears to fit neatly inside the skillet.

MAKES 4 SERVINGS
HANDS-ON TIME 20 MINUTES
TOTAL TIME 20 MINUTES

Tahini Falafel Lettuce Burgers
With Cucumber Salsa

FALAFEL BURGERS

2	green onions, chopped
3	cloves garlic, chopped
1	540 ml can chickpeas, drained and rinsed
¼ cup	chopped fresh cilantro
1	egg
1 tsp	each ground cumin and chili powder
¼ tsp	each salt and pepper
¼ cup	chickpea flour or all-purpose flour
4 tsp	vegetable oil
4	large green or red lettuce leaves, separated
4 tsp	tahini

CUCUMBER SALSA

2	plum tomatoes, seeded and diced
1 cup	diced seeded English cucumber (about half cucumber)
1 tbsp	chopped fresh mint
2 tsp	white wine vinegar
pinch	each salt and pepper

FALAFEL BURGERS In food processor, pulse green onions with garlic until finely chopped. Add chickpeas, cilantro, egg, cumin, chili powder, salt and pepper; pulse into fine paste. Add chickpea flour; pulse until combined. Shape into 4 balls; flatten each to ¾-inch thickness.

In large nonstick skillet, heat oil over medium heat; cook falafel, turning once, until golden, 6 to 8 minutes. Arrange 1 falafel in each lettuce leaf; drizzle with tahini.

CUCUMBER SALSA While falafel are cooking, in bowl, stir together tomatoes, cucumber, mint, vinegar, salt and pepper. Serve over falafel.

NUTRITIONAL INFORMATION PER SERVING about 242 cal, 10 g pro, 11 g total fat (1 g sat. fat), 27 g carb (7 g dietary fibre, 6 g sugar), 48 mg chol, 348 mg sodium, 374 mg potassium. % RDI: 9% calcium, 20% iron, 17% vit A, 12% vit C, 35% folate.

TEST KITCHEN TIP

If you don't mind the extra calories, you can use pitas or hamburger buns for a more traditional veggie burger.

Lemony Ravioli
With Sun-Dried Tomatoes

MAKES 2 TO 3 SERVINGS
HANDS-ON TIME 15 MINUTES
TOTAL TIME 20 MINUTES

In large pot of boiling salted water, cook pasta according to package directions. Reserving ⅓ cup of the cooking liquid, drain.

In large nonstick skillet, heat butter and oil over medium heat until butter is melted; cook sun-dried tomatoes and garlic, stirring often, until fragrant, 2 to 3 minutes. Add pasta, Parmesan, parsley, lemon zest, lemon juice and capers; cook, stirring gently, for 2 minutes. Stir in enough of the reserved cooking liquid to coat.

NUTRITIONAL INFORMATION PER EACH OF 3 SERVINGS about 322 cal, 10 g pro, 18 g total fat (6 g sat. fat), 32 g carb (3 g dietary fibre, 3 g sugar), 39 mg chol, 779 mg sodium, 211 mg potassium. % RDI: 14% calcium, 18% iron, 9% vit A, 35% vit C, 5% folate.

250 g	fresh vegetable- or cheese-filled ravioli
1 tbsp	butter
1 tbsp	olive oil
¼ cup	thinly sliced drained oil-packed sun-dried tomatoes
2	cloves garlic, minced
¼ cup	grated Parmesan cheese
¼ cup	chopped fresh parsley
1 tbsp	thinly sliced lemon zest
3 tbsp	lemon juice
1 tbsp	capers, drained and rinsed

TEST KITCHEN TIP

Capers and caper berries come from a Mediterranean shrub, harvested at different stages. The tiny unopened buds, brined and pickled, give us capers. Left unpicked, the buds will produce flowers and then berries. Caper berries are also pickled; their texture is similar to olives.

MAKES 4 TO 6 SERVINGS
HANDS-ON TIME 15 MINUTES
TOTAL TIME 40 MINUTES

Kale & Sweet Potato Frittata

10	eggs
3 tbsp	water
¾ tsp	salt
¼ tsp	pepper
1	small sweet potato
2 tbsp	olive oil, divided
2 cups	packed kale, torn
2	green onions, chopped
½ cup	crumbled feta cheese
	microgreens (optional)

Position rack in top third of oven; preheat to 400°F. In large bowl, whisk eggs; whisk in water, salt and pepper. Set aside.

Halve sweet potato lengthwise; cut crosswise into ¼-inch thick slices to make 2 cups. In 10-inch cast-iron or ovenproof skillet, heat 1 tbsp of the oil over medium heat; cook sweet potato in single layer, flipping once, until fork-tender, about 8 minutes. Transfer to plate.

Add remaining 1 tbsp oil to pan; cook kale and green onions, stirring occasionally, until kale is wilted, about 2 minutes.

Return sweet potato to pan; stir to combine. Pour in egg mixture; cook, running spatula along edge to let egg mixture flow underneath, until edge starts to pull away from pan, 4 to 5 minutes. Sprinkle with feta.

Bake until light golden and set, about 8 minutes; broil for 1 minute. Cut into wedges; top with microgreens (if using).

NUTRITIONAL INFORMATION PER EACH OF 6 SERVINGS about 236 cal, 13 g pro, 16 g total fat (5 g sat. fat), 10 g carb (2 g dietary fibre, 5 g sugar), 331 mg chol, 535 mg sodium, 330 mg potassium. % RDI: 11% calcium, 13% iron, 107% vit A, 20% vit C, 26% folate.

MAKE IT A MEAL

Kale & Sweet Potato Frittata	236 cal
Add: ¾ cup steamed sliced zucchini	15 cal
1 dinner roll	85 cal
Total	**336 cal**

Sticky Tofu & Broccoli Stir-Fry

MAKES 4 SERVINGS
HANDS-ON TIME 25 MINUTES
TOTAL TIME 30 MINUTES

In bowl, stir together hoisin sauce, soy sauce, chili sauce, vinegar and ginger. Set aside.

Remove gills from mushrooms. Halve caps; thinly slice. Cut tofu into 1-inch cubes; pat dry with paper towel. Using fine-mesh sieve, dust tofu with cornstarch, turning to coat.

In large nonstick skillet or wok, heat 2 tbsp of the oil over high heat; stir-fry tofu, turning often, until golden, 4 to 6 minutes. Transfer to bowl; toss with half of the hoisin mixture. Set aside.

Add remaining 1 tbsp oil to pan; stir-fry mushrooms and broccoli for 2 minutes. Add garlic, yellow pepper and red onion; stir-fry for 2 minutes. Add remaining hoisin mixture; stir-fry until broccoli is tender-crisp, 1 to 2 minutes. Stir in tofu and basil (if using).

NUTRITIONAL INFORMATION PER SERVING about 308 cal, 17 g pro, 18 g total fat (2 g sat. fat), 24 g carb (4 g dietary fibre, 10 g sugar), 0 mg chol, 493 mg sodium, 705 mg potassium. % RDI: 18% calcium, 21% iron, 23% vit A, 198% vit C, 35% folate.

¼ cup	hoisin sauce
1 tbsp	sodium-reduced soy sauce
1 tbsp	Asian chili sauce (such as sriracha)
1 tbsp	rice vinegar or cider vinegar
1 tsp	ground ginger
2	large portobello mushrooms, stemmed
1	350 g pkg extra-firm tofu, drained
2 tsp	cornstarch
3 tbsp	vegetable oil, divided
1	head broccoli, cut in florets (about 4 cups)
3	cloves garlic, minced
1	sweet yellow pepper, thinly sliced
half	red onion, thinly sliced
1 cup	fresh basil leaves (optional)

MAKES 4 SERVINGS
HANDS-ON TIME 20 MINUTES
TOTAL TIME 25 MINUTES

Vegetarian Ma Po Tofu

1 cup	20-minute whole grain brown rice
1 tbsp	vegetable oil or sesame oil
1	carrot, quartered lengthwise and cut crosswise in ½-inch thick pieces
4	green onions, sliced and divided
1 tbsp	minced peeled fresh ginger
120 g	green beans, trimmed and cut in 1-inch lengths
100 g	shiitake mushrooms, stemmed and sliced
2 tbsp	black bean garlic sauce
2 tsp	Korean hot pepper paste (gochujang)
1 tbsp	cornstarch
1 cup	water (approx)
1	454 g pkg medium-firm tofu, cut in ¾-inch cubes

In saucepan, cook rice according to package directions.

Meanwhile, in large nonstick skillet or wok, heat oil over medium-high heat; stir-fry carrot, three-quarters of the green onions and the ginger until carrot is beginning to soften, about 4 minutes. Add green beans and mushrooms; stir-fry until green beans are beginning to soften, about 3 minutes. Stir in black bean garlic sauce and hot pepper paste; cook, stirring, until fragrant, about 1 minute.

Whisk cornstarch with 1 cup water; stir into vegetable mixture. Bring to boil; cook, stirring, until thickened, about 1 minute. Reduce heat to medium. Add tofu; cook, stirring gently, until tofu is coated and warmed through, about 3 minutes. If necessary, add water, 1 tbsp at a time, to reach desired consistency.

Divide rice among serving bowls; top with ma po tofu. Sprinkle with remaining green onions.

NUTRITIONAL INFORMATION PER SERVING about 370 cal, 26 g pro, 15 g total fat (1 g sat. fat), 52 g carb (4 g dietary fibre, 6 g sugar), 0 mg chol, 226 mg sodium, 470 mg potassium. % RDI: 18% calcium, 25% iron, 114% vit A, 8% vit C, 27% folate.

TEST KITCHEN TIP

Korean hot pepper paste isn't traditionally found in ma po tofu recipes, but it adds an umami-rich kick. Look for it in small plastic tubs in the Asian section of your grocery store, or substitute with 1 tsp sriracha.

Lentil & Sweet Potato Salad
With Halloumi

MAKES 4 SERVINGS
HANDS-ON TIME 20 MINUTES
TOTAL TIME 50 MINUTES

SHALLOT VINAIGRETTE In small bowl, whisk together shallot, oil, lemon juice, mustard, salt and pepper. Set aside.

SALAD Preheat oven to 425°F. In saucepan, bring lentils and water to boil. Reduce heat, cover and simmer until lentils are tender, 15 to 20 minutes; drain. Let cool slightly.

While lentils are cooking, in large bowl, toss together sweet potato, oil, garlic powder, paprika, pepper and salt. Arrange in single layer on greased baking sheet. Bake, turning once, until tender, 15 to 18 minutes. Scrape onto plate; set aside. Wipe pan clean.

Arrange halloumi in single layer on same pan; broil until golden, about 3 minutes. Transfer to cutting board; coarsely chop.

In clean large bowl, combine lentils, sweet potato, halloumi and cilantro. Drizzle with Shallot Vinaigrette; toss to coat.

NUTRITIONAL INFORMATION PER SERVING about 382 cal, 16 g pro, 16 g total fat (6 g sat. fat), 45 g carb (8 g dietary fibre, 10 g sugar), 25 mg chol, 357 mg sodium, 701 mg potassium. % RDI: 18% calcium, 31% iron, 222% vit A, 35% vit C, 81% folate.

SHALLOT VINAIGRETTE

1	shallot, minced
2 tbsp	extra-virgin olive oil
4 tsp	lemon juice
1 tsp	Dijon mustard
pinch	each salt and pepper

SALAD

⅔ cup	dried green lentils, rinsed
3 cups	water
4 cups	cubed peeled sweet potato
2 tsp	extra-virgin olive oil
1½ tsp	garlic powder
1 tsp	smoked paprika
¼ tsp	pepper
pinch	salt
4	slices halloumi cheese (about 100 g total)
¼ cup	chopped fresh cilantro

TEST KITCHEN TIP

Halloumi, a traditional cheese from Cyprus, holds its shape when heated, making it a Test Kitchen favourite for broiling and grilling.

One-Pot Quinoa Chili

MAKES 6 SERVINGS
HANDS-ON TIME 10 MINUTES
TOTAL TIME 35 MINUTES

2 tsp	olive oil
1	onion, chopped
3	cloves garlic, minced
1	156 ml can tomato paste
2 tbsp	ground cumin
1 tbsp	each chili powder and smoked paprika
4 cups	vegetable broth
1	796 ml can diced tomatoes
¾ cup	quinoa, rinsed
1	540 ml can black beans, drained and rinsed
1	540 ml can kidney beans, drained and rinsed
1 cup	frozen corn
3 tbsp	fresh cilantro, chopped
1 tsp	pepper
½ tsp	salt (optional)

In Dutch oven or large heavy-bottomed pot, heat oil over medium heat; cook onion, stirring frequently, until softened, about 5 minutes. Add garlic; cook, stirring occasionally, until fragrant, about 1 minute.

Stir in tomato paste, cumin, chili powder and paprika; cook for 2 minutes. Add broth and tomatoes; bring to boil over high heat, stirring frequently.

Stir in quinoa; reduce heat to low, cover and simmer for 15 minutes. Add black beans, kidney beans, corn, cilantro, pepper and salt (if using); simmer, uncovered, until quinoa is fluffy, 8 to 10 minutes.

Ladle into serving bowls; garnish with toppings such as sliced avocado, thinly sliced red onion, sliced radish, pickled jalapeño peppers or coconut crema (optional).

NUTRITIONAL INFORMATION PER SERVING about 334 cal, 17 g pro, 5 g total fat (1 g sat. fat), 62 g carb (16 g dietary fibre, 13 g sugar), 3 mg chol, 1,084 mg sodium, 1,204 mg potassium. % RDI: 14% calcium, 53% iron, 19% vit A, 50% vit C, 47% folate.

TEST KITCHEN TIP

To make coconut crema, skim the solid cream from the top of canned coconut milk. Thin with enough lemon juice to make a drizzle.

Green Shakshuka

MAKES 6 SERVINGS
HANDS-ON TIME 30 MINUTES
TOTAL TIME 40 MINUTES

In large nonstick skillet, heat oil over medium heat; cook leek and jalapeño pepper, stirring occasionally, until softened, 3 to 4 minutes. Add garlic, cumin and salt; cook, stirring, until fragrant, about 30 seconds. Stir in kale and broth; cook until kale is wilted, about 4 minutes. Stir in spinach, 2 cups at a time; cook until wilted, about 2 minutes. Stir in parsley.

Using back of spoon, make 6 wells in kale mixture; crack 1 egg into each. Sprinkle with feta. Reduce heat to medium-low, cover and cook until egg whites are set but yolks are still slightly runny, about 10 minutes. Remove from heat; sprinkle with dill.

NUTRITIONAL INFORMATION PER SERVING about 169 cal, 12 g pro, 12 g total fat (4 g sat. fat), 7 g carb (2 g dietary fibre, 3 g sugar), 200 mg chol, 482 mg sodium, 349 mg potassium. % RDI: 13% calcium, 21% iron, 59% vit A, 37% vit C, 46% folate.

SERVE WITH
Cucumber Couscous Salad

In large heatproof bowl, cover 1 cup whole wheat couscous with 1 cup boiling water; let stand for 5 minutes. Fluff with fork; let cool. Add 2 cups diced English cucumber; ½ cup sliced radishes; and 2 green onions, sliced.

In small bowl, whisk together 3 tbsp vegetable oil; 2 tbsp lemon juice; 1 tbsp chopped fresh thyme; 1 clove garlic, minced; ½ tsp each cumin and salt; and ¼ tsp pepper. Toss dressing with salad. Sprinkle with ¼ cup pine nuts. Makes 6 servings.

NUTRITIONAL INFORMATION PER SERVING about 228 cal, 7 g pro, 11 g total fat (1 g sat. fat), 29 g carb (6 g dietary fibre), 0 mg chol, 198 mg sodium. % RDI: 3% calcium, 15% iron, 2% vit A, 13% vit C, 10% folate.

2 tbsp	olive oil
1	leek (white and light green parts only), halved lengthwise and thinly sliced crosswise (about 2 cups)
1	jalapeño pepper, halved, seeded and thinly sliced
2	cloves garlic, minced
1 tsp	ground cumin
¾ tsp	salt
6 cups	stemmed kale, coarsely chopped
1 cup	no-salt-added vegetable broth
10 cups	baby spinach
¼ cup	fresh parsley, coarsely chopped
6	eggs
⅓ cup	crumbled feta cheese
¼ cup	fresh dill, coarsely chopped

Baked Chilaquiles Verde
With Eggs

MAKES 6 SERVINGS
HANDS-ON TIME 10 MINUTES
TOTAL TIME 30 MINUTES

1 tbsp	olive oil
2	small zucchini, thinly sliced
¼ tsp	salt (optional)
4	green onions, sliced
1	430 ml jar tomatillo salsa or salsa verde, divided
250 g	unsalted corn tortilla chips (about 8 cups)
6	eggs
2 tbsp	crumbled feta cheese
¼ tsp	pepper
	chopped fresh cilantro (optional)
	avocado slices (optional)
	sour cream or yogurt (optional)

Preheat oven to 400°F. In large ovenproof skillet, heat oil over medium-high heat; cook zucchini and salt (if using) until slightly softened, 3 to 4 minutes. Stir in green onions; cook for 1 minute. Reduce heat to low; stir in 1½ cups of the salsa. Remove pan from heat; fold in tortilla chips until evenly coated.

Bake until tortilla chips in centre of pan are softened and chips around edge are crisp, about 10 minutes. Using spoon, make 6 wells in salsa mixture; crack 1 egg into each well. Continue to bake until egg whites are set but yolks are still runny, 8 to 10 minutes. Remove from oven. Sprinkle with feta and pepper; spoon remaining salsa over top. Serve immediately with cilantro, avocado and sour cream (if using).

NUTRITIONAL INFORMATION PER SERVING about 356 cal, 11 g pro, 19 g total fat (4 g sat. fat), 35 g carb (3 g dietary fibre, 7 g sugar), 196 mg chol, 914 mg sodium, 486 mg potassium. % RDI: 12% calcium, 15% iron, 23% vit A, 18% vit C, 27% folate.

TEST KITCHEN TIP

If you don't have green tomatillo salsa, you can also make a rosy version of this dish (called chilaquiles rojos) with tomato-based salsa and your favourite red veggies instead of zucchini and green onions. We suggest sweet red peppers and thinly sliced red onions.

Vegetarian Ramen Noodle Soup

MAKES 4 SERVINGS
HANDS-ON TIME 30 MINUTES
TOTAL TIME 30 MINUTES

In saucepan, heat oil over medium-high heat; cook garlic until fragrant, 2 minutes.

Add water and broth; bring to boil. Add mushrooms; reduce heat and simmer for 5 minutes. Stir in miso paste and soy sauce.

Meanwhile, in large pot of boiling water, cook noodles according to package directions; drain and divide among 4 large soup bowls. Top each with 2 egg halves. Ladle soup over top. Sprinkle with green onions and seaweed.

NUTRITIONAL INFORMATION PER SERVING about 284 cal, 15 g pro, 9 g total fat (3 g sat. fat), 39 g carb (3 g dietary fibre, 6 g sugar), 222 mg chol, 1,110 mg sodium, 287 mg potassium. % RDI: 6% calcium, 16% iron, 17% vit A, 7% vit C, 22% folate.

2 tsp	sesame oil
3	cloves garlic, minced
3 cups	water
1	900 ml pkg vegetable broth
225 g	shiitake mushrooms, stemmed and thinly sliced
4 tsp	miso paste
2 tsp	sodium-reduced soy sauce
280 g	fresh ramen noodles
4	hard-cooked eggs, peeled and halved
6	green onions, thinly sliced
1	strip (2 inches wide) roasted seaweed, cut crosswise in 8 strips

TEST KITCHEN TIP

You'll find fresh ramen noodles in the refrigerated Asian section of your grocery store, but you can also use rice vermicelli; look for noodles about ⅛ inch wide.

Vegetable Quinoa Soup

2 tsp	olive oil
1	onion, diced
2	cloves garlic, minced
1 cup	thinly sliced cremini mushrooms (about 115 g)
1	sweet potato (about 340 g), peeled and diced
3 cups	water
2 cups	sodium-reduced vegetable broth
½ cup	quinoa, rinsed
½ tsp	pepper
¼ tsp	salt
2 cups	stemmed kale, thinly sliced
1 tbsp	red wine vinegar

In large saucepan, heat oil over medium heat; cook onion and garlic, stirring occasionally, until softened, about 5 minutes.

Add mushrooms; cook, stirring occasionally, until beginning to soften, about 4 minutes. Stir in sweet potato, water, broth, quinoa, pepper and salt; bring to boil. Reduce heat to medium; cook until quinoa is tender, 10 to 12 minutes.

Stir in kale; cook until tender, about 4 minutes. Stir in vinegar.

NUTRITIONAL INFORMATION PER SERVING about 195 cal, 6 g pro, 5 g total fat (1 g sat. fat), 36 g carb (5 g dietary fibre, 7 g sugar), 0 mg chol, 194 mg sodium, 668 mg potassium. % RDI: 9% calcium, 24% iron, 164% vit A, 77% vit C, 15% folate.

TEST KITCHEN TIP

Quinoa is high in protein and iron. Rinsing it before cooking helps remove the natural saponin coating, which can cause a bitter flavour when cooked.

Cauliflower Corn Chowder

MAKES 6 SERVINGS
HANDS-ON TIME 30 MINUTES
TOTAL TIME 30 MINUTES

In Dutch oven or large heavy-bottomed pot, heat oil over medium-high heat; cook onion, garlic and 2 tsp of the thyme, stirring, just until onion is softened, about 3 minutes. Stir in corn kernels, cauliflower, broth, water, salt and pepper; bring to boil. Reduce heat, cover and simmer until cauliflower is tender, about 8 minutes.

In blender, purée 4 cups of the soup until smooth; return to pot. Whisk milk with flour; stir into soup. Add red pepper; bring to boil. Reduce heat; simmer, uncovered and stirring occasionally, just until red pepper is tender and soup is slightly thickened, about 2 minutes. Stir in lemon juice. Sprinkle with remaining 1 tsp thyme.

NUTRITIONAL INFORMATION PER SERVING about 198 cal, 7 g pro, 7 g total fat (1 g sat. fat), 31 g carb (6 g dietary fibre, 9 g sugar), 5 mg chol, 317 mg sodium, 446 mg potassium. % RDI: 10% calcium, 10% iron, 11% vit A, 133% vit C, 38% folate.

VARIATION

Chicken & Cauliflower Corn Chowder
Stir in 2 cups chopped cooked chicken breast along with the red pepper.

2 tbsp	olive oil
1	onion, diced
4	cloves garlic, minced
1 tbsp	chopped fresh thyme, divided
1½ cups	fresh or frozen corn kernels (about 3 corncobs)
1	small head cauliflower, cut in bite-size florets (about 6 cups)
3 cups	sodium-reduced vegetable broth
½ cup	water
½ tsp	salt
¼ tsp	pepper
1½ cups	milk
3 tbsp	all-purpose flour
1	sweet red pepper, diced
2 tbsp	lemon juice

MAKES 4 TO 6 SERVINGS
HANDS-ON TIME 20 MINUTES
TOTAL TIME 30 MINUTES

Hot & Sour Soup

2 tbsp	vegetable oil
3	green onions (white and green parts separated), thinly sliced
2	cloves garlic, minced
1	1-inch piece ginger, peeled and julienned (about 1 tbsp)
½ tsp	hot pepper flakes
2 cups	sliced stemmed shiitake mushrooms
1	carrot, halved lengthwise and thinly sliced
1	350 g pkg extra-firm tofu, drained and cut in ½-inch cubes
7 cups	sodium-reduced vegetable broth, warmed
2 tbsp	water
1 tbsp	cornstarch
1 cup	thinly sliced trimmed snow peas
2 tbsp	white vinegar
1 tbsp	sodium-reduced soy sauce
1 tsp	granulated sugar
2	eggs, lightly beaten

In large saucepan, heat oil over medium heat; cook white parts of green onions, the garlic, ginger and hot pepper flakes for 1 minute. Increase heat to medium-high. Add mushrooms and carrot; cook until carrot begins to soften, about 3 minutes. Add tofu; cook, stirring often, for 3 minutes. Increase heat to high. Add broth; cover and bring to boil. Reduce heat to medium; simmer, uncovered, for 10 minutes.

Whisk water with cornstarch; stir into broth mixture. Increase heat to high. Stir in snow peas, vinegar, soy sauce and sugar; bring to boil. Reduce heat to medium; simmer until slightly thickened, about 1 minute. Remove from heat; drizzle in eggs in thin steady stream, stirring constantly. Sprinkle with green parts of green onions; serve immediately.

NUTRITIONAL INFORMATION PER EACH OF 6 SERVINGS about 199 cal, 12 g pro, 11 g total fat (1 g sat. fat), 14 g carb (3 g dietary fibre, 6 g sugar), 64 mg chol, 317 mg sodium, 300 mg potassium. % RDI: 14% calcium, 18% iron, 57% vit A, 13% vit C, 16% folate.

MAKE IT A MEAL

Hot & Sour Soup	199 cal
Add: Napa Cabbage Salad With Ginger Dressing (page 141)	33 cal
Total	**232 cal**

Mixed Greens
With Maple Soy
Vinaigrette

Mixed Greens With Maple Soy Vinaigrette

MAKES 4 SERVINGS
HANDS-ON TIME 5 MINUTES
TOTAL TIME 5 MINUTES

2 tbsp	vegetable oil
1 tbsp	rice vinegar
2 tsp	soy sauce
2 tsp	maple syrup
1 tsp	sesame oil
8 cups	lightly packed mixed salad greens
1	carrot, grated

In large bowl, whisk together vegetable oil, vinegar, soy sauce, maple syrup and sesame oil.

Add mixed greens and carrot; toss to coat.

NUTRITIONAL INFORMATION PER SERVING about 107 cal, 2 g pro, 8 g total fat (1 g sat. fat), 8 g carb (2 g dietary fibre), 0 mg chol, 191 mg sodium, 400 mg potassium. % RDI: 7% calcium, 6% iron, 48% vit A, 27% vit C, 44% folate.

Mixed Greens With Lemon Chive Dressing

MAKES 6 SERVINGS
HANDS-ON TIME 5 MINUTES
TOTAL TIME 5 MINUTES

2 tbsp	vegetable oil
1½ tbsp	lemon juice
1 tbsp	chopped fresh chives or green onion
¼ tsp	Dijon mustard
¼ tsp	salt
pinch	pepper
half	bulb fennel, trimmed, cored and thinly sliced lengthwise
4 cups	torn mixed salad greens

In bowl, whisk together oil, lemon juice, chives, mustard, salt and pepper.

In large bowl, toss fennel with 1 tbsp of the dressing. Add greens and remaining dressing; toss together.

NUTRITIONAL INFORMATION PER SERVING about 53 cal, 1 g pro, 5 g total fat (trace sat. fat), 3 g carb (1 g dietary fibre), 0 mg chol, 118 mg sodium. % RDI: 3% calcium, 3% iron, 8% vit A, 15% vit C, 17% folate.

Arugula & Mushroom Salad

MAKES 4 TO 6 SERVINGS
HANDS-ON TIME 5 MINUTES
TOTAL TIME 5 MINUTES

2 tbsp	extra-virgin olive oil
1 tsp	lemon zest
5 tsp	lemon juice
pinch	each salt and pepper
1	142 g pkg baby arugula (about 10 cups)
2	cremini or white mushrooms, thinly sliced
¼ cup	shaved Parmesan cheese

In large bowl, whisk together oil, lemon zest, lemon juice, salt and pepper. Add arugula, mushrooms and Parmesan; toss to coat.

NUTRITIONAL INFORMATION PER EACH OF 6 SERVINGS about 59 cal, 2 g pro, 5 g total fat (1 g sat. fat), 2 g carb (trace dietary fibre, 1 g sugar), 1 mg chol, 84 mg sodium, 41 mg potassium. % RDI: 6% calcium, 3% iron, 6% vit A, 9% vit C, 1% folate.

Make-Ahead Fennel & Parmesan Slaw

MAKES 6 TO 8 SERVINGS
HANDS-ON TIME 10 MINUTES
TOTAL TIME 4¼ HOURS

½ tsp	grated lemon zest
3 tbsp	each lemon juice and extra-virgin olive oil
¼ tsp	salt
pinch	pepper
1	bulb fennel, trimmed, cored and thinly sliced
2 tsp	coarsely chopped fennel fronds
half	small Vidalia onion, thinly sliced
½ cup	shaved Parmesan cheese

In large bowl, combine lemon zest, lemon juice, oil, salt and pepper.

Add fennel, fennel fronds and onion; toss to combine. Cover and refrigerate for 4 hours. *(Make-ahead: Refrigerate for up to 24 hours.)*

Just before serving, add Parmesan and toss to combine.

NUTRITIONAL INFORMATION PER EACH OF 8 SERVINGS about 85 cal, 3 g pro, 7 g total fat (2 g sat. fat), 4 g carb (1 g dietary fibre, 1 g sugar), 5 mg chol, 198 mg sodium, 146 mg potassium. % RDI: 9% calcium, 2% iron, 1% vit A, 12% vit C, 5% folate.

Tomato & Feta Salad

MAKES 8 SERVINGS
HANDS-ON TIME 5 MINUTES
TOTAL TIME 5 MINUTES

8	small tomatoes, cored and cut in wedges
quarter	English cucumber, thinly sliced
375 g	feta cheese, crumbled
¼ cup	extra-virgin olive oil
12	sun-dried black olives
1 tbsp	chopped fresh parsley

In large bowl, toss together tomatoes, cucumber, feta, oil and olives. Sprinkle with parsley.

NUTRITIONAL INFORMATION PER SERVING about 194 cal, 7 g pro, 17 g total fat (8 g sat. fat), 5 g carb (1 g dietary fibre), 39 mg chol, 553 mg sodium. % RDI: 21% calcium, 6% iron, 9% vit A, 17% vit C, 10% folate.

Heirloom Tomato Salad

MAKES 4 SERVINGS
HANDS-ON TIME 5 MINUTES
TOTAL TIME 5 MINUTES

2 tbsp	extra-virgin olive oil
1 tbsp	sherry vinegar
pinch	each salt and pepper
450 g	halved or quartered mini heirloom tomatoes
1	rib celery, thinly sliced
⅓ cup	chopped fresh parsley

In large bowl, whisk together oil, vinegar, salt and pepper. Stir in tomatoes, celery and parsley; toss to combine.

NUTRITIONAL INFORMATION PER SERVING about 84 cal, 1 g pro, 7 g total fat (1 g sat. fat), 5 g carb (3 g sugar), 0 mg chol, 17 mg sodium. % RDI: 2% calcium, 5% iron, 14% vit A, 35% vit C, 13% folate.

Creamy Cucumber Salad

MAKES 4 SERVINGS
HANDS-ON TIME 5 MINUTES
TOTAL TIME 35 MINUTES

3 cups	thinly sliced peeled English cucumber
1 tsp	salt
½ cup	thinly sliced red onion
¼ cup	sour cream
1 tbsp	chopped fresh dill (or 1 tsp dried dillweed)
1 tbsp	white wine vinegar
1 tsp	granulated sugar

In colander, sprinkle cucumber with salt; let stand to drain for 30 minutes. Pat dry.

Meanwhile, soak red onion in cold water for 15 minutes; drain and pat dry.

In bowl, whisk together sour cream, dill, vinegar and sugar. Add cucumber and onion; toss to coat.

NUTRITIONAL INFORMATION PER SERVING about 38 cal, 2 g pro, 1 g total fat (1 g sat. fat), 6 g carb (1 g dietary fibre), 2 mg chol, 302 mg sodium. % RDI: 4% calcium, 1% iron, 1% vit A, 7% vit C, 7% folate.

Cucumber Cilantro Salad

MAKES 4 SERVINGS
HANDS-ON TIME 5 MINUTES
TOTAL TIME 15 MINUTES

1	English cucumber, seeded and diced
⅓ cup	diced red onion
¼ cup	chopped fresh cilantro
1 tbsp	vegetable oil
¼ tsp	granulated sugar
pinch	each salt and pepper

In large bowl, toss together cucumber, red onion, cilantro, oil, sugar, salt and pepper. Let stand for 10 minutes before serving.

NUTRITIONAL INFORMATION PER SERVING about 49 cal, 1 g pro, 4 g total fat (trace sat. fat), 4 g carb (2 g sugar), 0 mg chol, 73 mg sodium. % RDI: 2% calcium, 2% iron, 2% vit A, 5% vit C, 5% folate.

Napa Cabbage Salad With Ginger Dressing

MAKES 4 SERVINGS
HANDS-ON TIME 5 MINUTES
TOTAL TIME 5 MINUTES

¼ cup	rice vinegar
1 tbsp	soy sauce
1 tsp	granulated sugar
½ tsp	grated fresh ginger
4 cups	finely shredded napa cabbage
1 cup	julienned carrots

Whisk together vinegar, soy sauce, sugar and ginger. Set aside.

In large bowl, toss cabbage with carrots; divide among serving plates. Drizzle with dressing.

NUTRITIONAL INFORMATION PER EACH OF 4 SERVINGS about 33 cal, 2 g pro, trace total fat (0 g sat. fat), 8 g carb (2 g dietary fibre), 0 mg chol, 254 mg sodium, 292 mg potassium. % RDI: 6% calcium, 3% iron, 53% vit A, 37% vit C, 30% folate.

Coleslaw
With Cider Vinaigrette

MAKES 10 TO 12 SERVINGS
HANDS-ON TIME 10 MINUTES
TOTAL TIME 2¼ HOURS

¼ cup	cider vinegar
1 tbsp	lemon juice
2 tsp	granulated sugar
½ tsp	salt
¼ tsp	pepper
⅓ cup	extra-virgin olive oil
10 cups	shredded Savoy cabbage
1½ cups	thinly sliced radishes
half	Vidalia or other sweet onion, thinly sliced
2 tbsp	chopped fresh parsley

In large bowl, whisk together vinegar, lemon juice, sugar, salt and pepper until sugar is dissolved, about 1 minute. Whisk in oil until blended.

Add cabbage, radishes, onion and parsley; toss to coat. Cover and refrigerate for 2 hours. *(Make-ahead: Refrigerate for up to 24 hours.)*

NUTRITIONAL INFORMATION PER EACH OF 12 SERVINGS about 78 cal, 1 g pro, 6 g total fat (1 g sat. fat), 6 g carb (1 g dietary fibre), 0 mg chol, 114 mg sodium, 204 mg potassium. % RDI: 3% calcium, 4% iron, 2% vit A, 38% vit C, 15% folate.

VARIATION

Tropical Coleslaw

Substitute lime juice for vinegar and fresh cilantro for parsley. Add 1 cup diced peeled cored pineapple and 1 mango, peeled, pitted and diced.

The Side-Dish Calorie Spectrum

Side dishes round out a meal, but if you're limiting calories, they can really add up.
Here are an assortment of common side dishes with calorie counts so you can mix and match with ease.

↑ Vegetables & Greens
↑ **Grains & Starches**

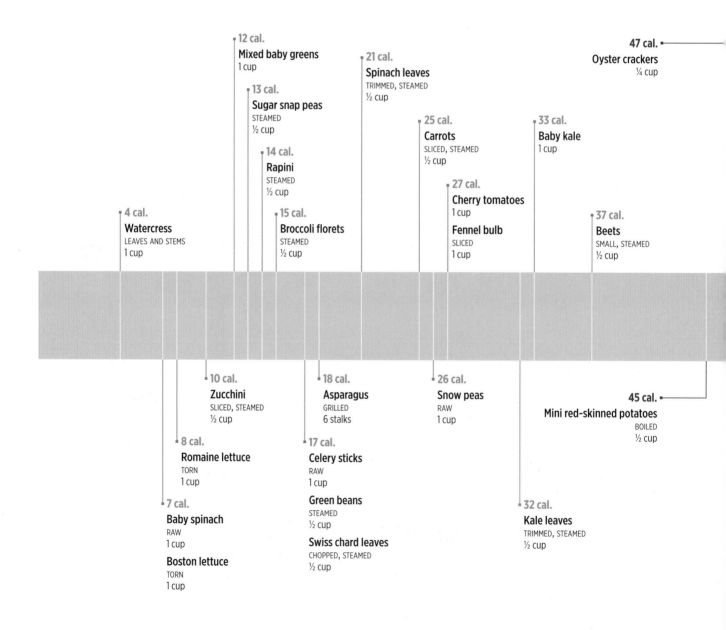

47 cal.
Oyster crackers
¼ cup

12 cal.
Mixed baby greens
1 cup

21 cal.
Spinach leaves
TRIMMED, STEAMED
½ cup

13 cal.
Sugar snap peas
STEAMED
½ cup

25 cal.
Carrots
SLICED, STEAMED
½ cup

33 cal.
Baby kale
1 cup

14 cal.
Rapini
STEAMED
½ cup

27 cal.
Cherry tomatoes
1 cup

Fennel bulb
SLICED
1 cup

4 cal.
Watercress
LEAVES AND STEMS
1 cup

15 cal.
Broccoli florets
STEAMED
½ cup

37 cal.
Beets
SMALL, STEAMED
½ cup

10 cal.
Zucchini
SLICED, STEAMED
½ cup

18 cal.
Asparagus
GRILLED
6 stalks

26 cal.
Snow peas
RAW
1 cup

45 cal.
Mini red-skinned potatoes
BOILED
½ cup

8 cal.
Romaine lettuce
TORN
1 cup

17 cal.
Celery sticks
RAW
1 cup

7 cal.
Baby spinach
RAW
1 cup

Green beans
STEAMED
½ cup

32 cal.
Kale leaves
TRIMMED, STEAMED
½ cup

Boston lettuce
TORN
1 cup

Swiss chard leaves
CHOPPED, STEAMED
½ cup

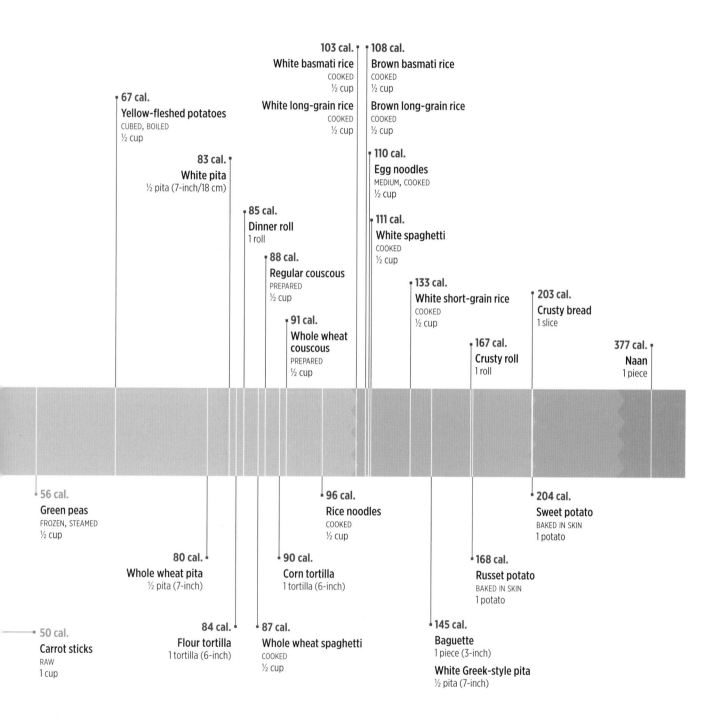

103 cal.
White basmati rice
COOKED
½ cup

White long-grain rice
COOKED
½ cup

108 cal.
Brown basmati rice
COOKED
½ cup

Brown long-grain rice
COOKED
½ cup

67 cal.
Yellow-fleshed potatoes
CUBED, BOILED
½ cup

110 cal.
Egg noodles
MEDIUM, COOKED
½ cup

83 cal.
White pita
½ pita (7-inch/18 cm)

111 cal.
White spaghetti
COOKED
½ cup

85 cal.
Dinner roll
1 roll

133 cal.
White short-grain rice
COOKED
½ cup

203 cal.
Crusty bread
1 slice

88 cal.
Regular couscous
PREPARED
½ cup

91 cal.
Whole wheat
couscous
PREPARED
½ cup

167 cal.
Crusty roll
1 roll

377 cal.
Naan
1 piece

56 cal.
Green peas
FROZEN, STEAMED
½ cup

96 cal.
Rice noodles
COOKED
½ cup

204 cal.
Sweet potato
BAKED IN SKIN
1 potato

80 cal.
Whole wheat pita
½ pita (7-inch)

90 cal.
Corn tortilla
1 tortilla (6-inch)

168 cal.
Russet potato
BAKED IN SKIN
1 potato

50 cal.
Carrot sticks
RAW
1 cup

84 cal.
Flour tortilla
1 tortilla (6-inch)

87 cal.
Whole wheat spaghetti
COOKED
½ cup

145 cal.
Baguette
1 piece (3-inch)

White Greek-style pita
½ pita (7-inch)

MAKES 16 SERVINGS
HANDS-ON TIME 1 HOUR
STANDING TIME 30 MINUTES
TOTAL TIME 1½ HOURS

Crêpes Suzette
With Sake-Soaked Oranges

SAKE-SOAKED ORANGES

2 tbsp	sake
¼ cup	granulated sugar
4	oranges, segmented

CRÊPES

2 cups	all-purpose flour
¼ cup	granulated sugar
2 cups	2% milk
4	large eggs
2 tsp	vanilla
2 tbsp	unsalted butter, melted

SUZETTE SAUCE

1⅓ cups	granulated sugar
¼ cup	water
1 cup	orange juice

ASSEMBLY

¼ cup	orange-flavoured liqueur

SAKE-SOAKED ORANGES In large microwaveable bowl, combine sake with sugar. Microwave on medium until sugar is dissolved, 45 to 60 seconds. Add oranges; stir to coat. Set aside.

CRÊPES In large bowl, whisk together flour and sugar. In separate bowl, whisk together milk, eggs and vanilla; pour over flour mixture, whisking until smooth. Strain through fine-mesh sieve into clean bowl; cover and let stand at room temperature for 30 minutes.

Heat 8-inch nonstick skillet or crêpe pan over medium-low heat; brush lightly with some of the butter. Pour scant ¼ cup of the batter into pan, swirling to coat bottom; cook, turning once when edge begins to curl, until light golden, 2 to 3 minutes. Transfer to plate; cover to keep warm. Repeat with remaining butter and batter.

SUZETTE SAUCE In heavy-bottomed saucepan, stir sugar with water over medium-high heat just until sugar is dissolved. Boil, without stirring but brushing down side of pan with pastry brush dipped in water, until mixture turns light amber, 9 to 11 minutes. Remove from heat. Averting face to avoid any spatters, stir in orange juice until smooth. Return pan to medium-high heat; cook, stirring occasionally, until mixture is reduced to 1¼ cups, 6 to 8 minutes. Transfer to heatproof bowl.

ASSEMBLY In large skillet, heat Suzette Sauce over medium heat for 1 minute. Reduce heat to low; add 1 crêpe, turning to coat. Using tongs, fold crêpe into quarters; transfer to large serving platter or roasting pan. Repeat with remaining crêpes. Drain orange segments; place over crêpes.

In small saucepan, heat orange-flavoured liqueur over medium heat for 1 minute; remove from heat. Using long match or barbecue lighter, ignite; while flaming, pour over crêpes. When flame goes out, serve immediately.

NUTRITIONAL INFORMATION PER SERVING about 183 cal, 5 g pro, 4 g total fat (2 g sat. fat), 31 g carb (1 g dietary fibre, 19 g sugar), 54 mg chol, 32 mg sodium, 116 mg potassium. % RDI: 5% calcium, 7% iron, 6% vit A, 18% vit C, 16% folate.

Creamy Peach Sherbet

MAKES 8 TO 10 SERVINGS
HANDS-ON TIME 30 MINUTES
FREEZING TIME 4 HOURS
REFRIGERATING TIME 1 HOUR
TOTAL TIME 6 HOURS

Score an X in bottom of each peach. In saucepan of boiling water, cook peaches until peels begin to loosen, about 30 seconds. Transfer to bowl of ice water and chill for 1 minute; drain. Using paring knife, peel off skins. Remove pits and dice flesh to yield 4 cups.

In saucepan, cook peaches and sugar over medium-high heat, stirring frequently, until peaches are softened, liquid has thickened and mixture reaches jam-like consistency, about 7 minutes. Scrape into blender; purée until smooth. Let cool slightly, about 5 minutes.

In large bowl, stir together peach mixture, milk, cream, vanilla and salt. Place plastic wrap directly on surface of mixture. Refrigerate until chilled, about 1 hour.

Process in ice cream machine according to manufacturer's directions. Spoon into large airtight freezer-safe container. Freeze until firm, about 4 hours.

1.2 kg	ripe peaches (about 6)
½ cup	granulated sugar
1⅓ cups	milk
⅔ cup	35% cream
1 tsp	vanilla
¼ tsp	salt

NUTRITIONAL INFORMATION PER EACH OF 10 SERVINGS about 138 cal, 2 g pro, 6 g total fat (4 g sat. fat), 20 g carb (2 g dietary fibre, 18 g sugar), 23 mg chol, 78 mg sodium, 211 mg potassium. % RDI: 5% calcium, 1% iron, 10% vit A, 7% vit C, 2% folate.

TEST KITCHEN TIP

Freestone peaches, as their name suggests, are easier to pit than clingstone peaches, which are available earlier in the season. Either type will work in this recipe; for best flavour, be sure the peaches are ripe.

MAKES 8 SERVINGS
HANDS-ON TIME 10 MINUTES
FREEZING TIME 8 HOURS
TOTAL TIME 8½ HOURS

Grapefruit & Tangerine Sorbet

3 cups	water
1½ cups	granulated sugar
1	strip each grapefruit zest and tangerine zest
2 cups	red grapefruit juice
1 cup	tangerine juice

In saucepan, bring water and sugar to boil over high heat, stirring until sugar is dissolved. Remove from heat; stir in grapefruit and tangerine zest. Cover and steep for 10 minutes. Stir in grapefruit and tangerine juice. Strain to remove zest and pulp.

Pour into 13- x 9-inch metal cake pan; freeze until firm, 4 to 6 hours. Break into chunks; purée in food processor. (Or freeze in ice cream machine according to manufacturer's directions.) Pack into airtight container; freeze until firm, about 4 hours.

Let sorbet stand in refrigerator for 10 minutes to soften before serving.

NUTRITIONAL INFORMATION PER SERVING about 183 cal, 1 g pro, trace total fat (0 g sat. fat), 46 g carb (0 g dietary fibre), 0 mg chol, 3 mg sodium. % RDI: 1% calcium, 1% iron, 3% vit A, 65% vit C, 7% folate.

VARIATIONS

Lemon Sorbet
Increase sugar to 3 cups. Replace grapefruit and tangerine zest and juice with lemon zest and juice.

Tangerine Sorbet
Replace grapefruit zest and grapefruit juice with tangerine zest and juice.

Creamy Lemon Coconut Macaroon Tart

Page 154

MAKES 16 SERVINGS
HANDS-ON TIME 30 MINUTES
REFRIGERATING TIME 8 HOURS
TOTAL TIME 10½ HOURS

Preheat oven to 350°F. In food processor, pulse 1¾ cups of the shredded coconut into coarse crumbs. In bowl, whisk egg whites with cornstarch until foamy; stir in coconut crumbs. Press into lightly greased 9-inch springform pan. Bake until firm, 12 to 14 minutes. Let cool completely.

In bowl, whisk together condensed milk, lemon juice, eggs and vanilla; pour over crust. Bake in 350°F oven until set, about 20 minutes. Let cool completely.

In separate bowl, beat cream cheese until smooth. Gradually beat in coconut milk. Beat in icing sugar and coconut extract until smooth. Pour over lemon layer. Refrigerate until set, about 8 hours. *(Make-ahead: Cover loosely with plastic wrap; refrigerate for up to 24 hours.)*

Run knife around edge of tart; remove from pan. Press remaining ¼ cup shredded coconut onto edge of tart.

2 cups	sweetened shredded coconut, toasted and divided
2	egg whites
1 tbsp	cornstarch
⅔ cup	sweetened condensed milk
½ cup	lemon juice
3	eggs
½ tsp	vanilla
1	250 g pkg cream cheese, softened
½ cup	coconut milk
½ cup	icing sugar
¼ tsp	coconut extract

NUTRITIONAL INFORMATION PER SERVING about 200 cal, 4 g pro, 13 g total fat (9 g sat. fat), 18 g carb (trace dietary fibre, 17 g sugar), 56 mg chol, 118 mg sodium, 148 mg potassium. % RDI: 5% calcium, 5% iron, 9% vit A, 3% vit C, 5% folate.

TEST KITCHEN TIP

To toast shredded coconut, add to a dry skillet over medium-low heat and cook, stirring often, until golden, about 5 minutes.

MAKES 6 ICE POPS
HANDS-ON TIME 10 MINUTES
FREEZING TIME 6 HOURS
TOTAL TIME 6½ HOURS

Yogurt Berry Ice Pops

1½ cups	blackberries, halved
2 tbsp	granulated sugar
2 cups	2% yogurt
¼ cup	liquid honey
¾ cup	granola, divided

In small bowl, stir blackberries with sugar until coated. Let stand, stirring occasionally, until syrupy, about 15 minutes.

In separate bowl, stir yogurt with honey until smooth. Alternately spoon yogurt and blackberry mixtures into 6 ice pop moulds, leaving ½ inch headspace; top each with 2 tsp of the granola. Insert pop sticks into centres. Freeze until firm, about 6 hours.

Remove from moulds; serve with remaining granola for dipping.

NUTRITIONAL INFORMATION PER ICE POP about 192 cal, 7 g pro, 5 g total fat (1 g sat. fat), 32 g carb (3 g dietary fibre, 26 g sugar), 5 mg chol, 66 mg sodium, 330 mg potassium. % RDI: 16% calcium, 6% iron, 2% vit A, 11% vit C, 13% folate.

TEST KITCHEN TIP

You can swap out the blackberries for any fresh berries that are in season.

Creamy Lemon Coconut
Macaroon Tart
Page 151

About Our Nutrition Information

To meet nutrient needs each day, moderately active women aged 25 to 49 need about 1,900 calories, 51 g protein, 261 g carbohydrate, 25 to 35 g fibre and not more than 63 g total fat (21 g saturated fat). Men and teenagers usually need more. Canadian sodium intake of approximately 3,500 mg daily should be reduced, whereas the intake of potassium from food sources should be increased to 4,700 mg per day. The percentage of recommended daily intake (% RDI) is based on the values used for Canadian food labels for calcium, iron, vitamins A and C, and folate.

Figures are rounded off. They are based on the first ingredient listed when there is a choice and do not include optional ingredients or those with no specified amounts.

Abbreviations

cal = calories   **pro** = protein   **carb** = carbohydrate   **sat. fat** = saturated fat   **chol** = cholesterol

Index

PHOTOGRAPHY

Jeff Coulson 30, 54, 58, 86, 110, 132, 138, 143

Angus Fergusson 13

Jim Norton 2, 7

Jodi Pudge 14, 35, 36, 69, 70, 116, 127, 154

Seuch and Beck 121

Ryan Szulc 148

Ronald Tsang 18, 29, 47, 53, 57, 63, 64, 73, 85, 96

James Tse 41, 74, 91, 98, 109, 115

Maya Visnyei 4, 8, 17, 25, 26, 42, 48, 79, 80, 92, 103, 104, 122, 128, 131, 137, 147, 153

FOOD STYLING

Ashley Denton 70, 91

Michael Elliott/Judy Inc. 13, 18, 57, 69, 79, 85, 109, 115, 116

Heather Eloph 110

David Grenier 14, 30, 35, 36, 63, 73, 86, 96, 104, 131, 132

Lucie Richard 41, 74, 98

Christopher St. Onge 64

Claire Stubbs 2, 4, 7, 8, 17, 25, 26, 29, 42, 47, 48, 53, 54, 80, 92, 103, 121, 122, 127, 128, 137, 147, 153

Melanie Stuparyk 58

Noah Witenoff 154

Nicole Young 138, 143, 148

PROP STYLING

Laura Branson 18, 35, 36, 41, 57, 69, 74, 85, 98, 109, 116, 127

Auralie Bryce 110

Alanna Davey 42, 80

Catherine Doherty 13, 30, 63, 73, 86, 91, 92, 96, 103, 104, 122, 131, 132, 137, 138, 143

Renée Drexler/Geary House 2, 7, 48, 147, 153

Jennifer Evans 14, 70, 115

Ann Marie Favot 25

Geary House 4, 8, 1, 2, 29, 47, 53, 79, 121, 128

Madeleine Johari 54, 64, 148

Sasha Seymour 58

Charlene Walton/Judy Inc. 154

Canadian Living

Complete your collection of Tested-Till-Perfect recipes!

The Ultimate Cookbook
The Special Occasions Cookbook
New Slow Cooker Favourites

The Complete Chicken Cookbook
The Complete Chocolate Cookbook
The Complete Preserving Cookbook
The Complete Vegetarian Cookbook

400-Calorie Dinners
Dinner in 30 Minutes or Less
Easy Cottage Cooking
Essential Barbecue
Essential Salads
Fish & Seafood
Healthy Family Meals
Make It Ahead!
Make It Chocolate!
Mediterranean Flavours
One Dish Favourites
Pasta & Noodles
Quick 400-Calorie Favourites
Sweet & Simple

The Affordable Feasts Collection
The Appetizer Collection
The Barbecue Collection
The International Collection
The One Dish Collection
The Slow Cooker Collection
The Vegetarian Collection

canadianliving.com/books